Devon and Cornwall

AA Publishing

Produced by AA Publishing

First published 1997. Reprinted 1998

Published by AA Publishing (a trading name of Automobile Association Developments Limited, whose registered office is Norfolk House, Priestley Road, Basingstoke, Hampshire RG24 9NY; registered number 1878835).

ISBN 0 7495 1491 4

A CIP catalogue record for this book is available from the British Library.

Designer: Jo Tapper

Colour separation by BTB, Digital Imaging, Whitchurch, Hampshire

Printed and bound by George Over Ltd, Rugby

DEVON AND CORNWALL

Devon is famous for its enchanting scenery and its long tradition of seafaring, in the heroic tradition of Sir Francis Drake and Sir John Hawkins, who sailed out in little ships to beat the overbearing galleons of the Spanish Armada. From the spacious and beautiful natural harbour of Plymouth Sound, the Pilgrim Fathers set sail for the New World; at Torbay the characteristic red cliffs of South Devon begin, which line the coast to the charming little Regency resort of Sidmouth. Inland is the county town and cathedral city of Exeter, once a Roman base; the spectacular coastline of North Devon includes the high cliffs of the Bristol Channel coast past Lynton and Combe Martin, the Victorian seaside resort of Ilfracombe, and jutting headlands protecting sandy beaches against the Atlantic tides at Woolacombe and Saunton.

Cornwall is separated from the rest of England by the River Tamar, and preserves an islated Celtic heritage. Tintagel is associated with the legend of King Arthur, and St Ia is said to have brought Christianity to St Ives in the Dark Ages, floating miraculously across the Irish Sea on a millstone. The sea has beaten the northern coast into a dramatic succession of great cliffs and headlands; stories of mermaids are told, and the engine houses of abandoned tin mines cling to the cliffs. The southern coast, the 'Cornish Riviera', is milder and more peaceful, with its fishing harbours with evocative names – Mevagissey and Mousehole, Mullion and Marazion. Offshore a causeway leads to St Michael's Mount. Inland, the granite landscape of Bodmin Moor rises to about 1,400ft (425m). Lands End is the most westerly point on the English mainland. About 28 miles (45km) further out lie the Isles of Scilly, famous both for spring flowers and shipwrecks. Truro is the county town, famous for its stunning 19th-century cathedral.

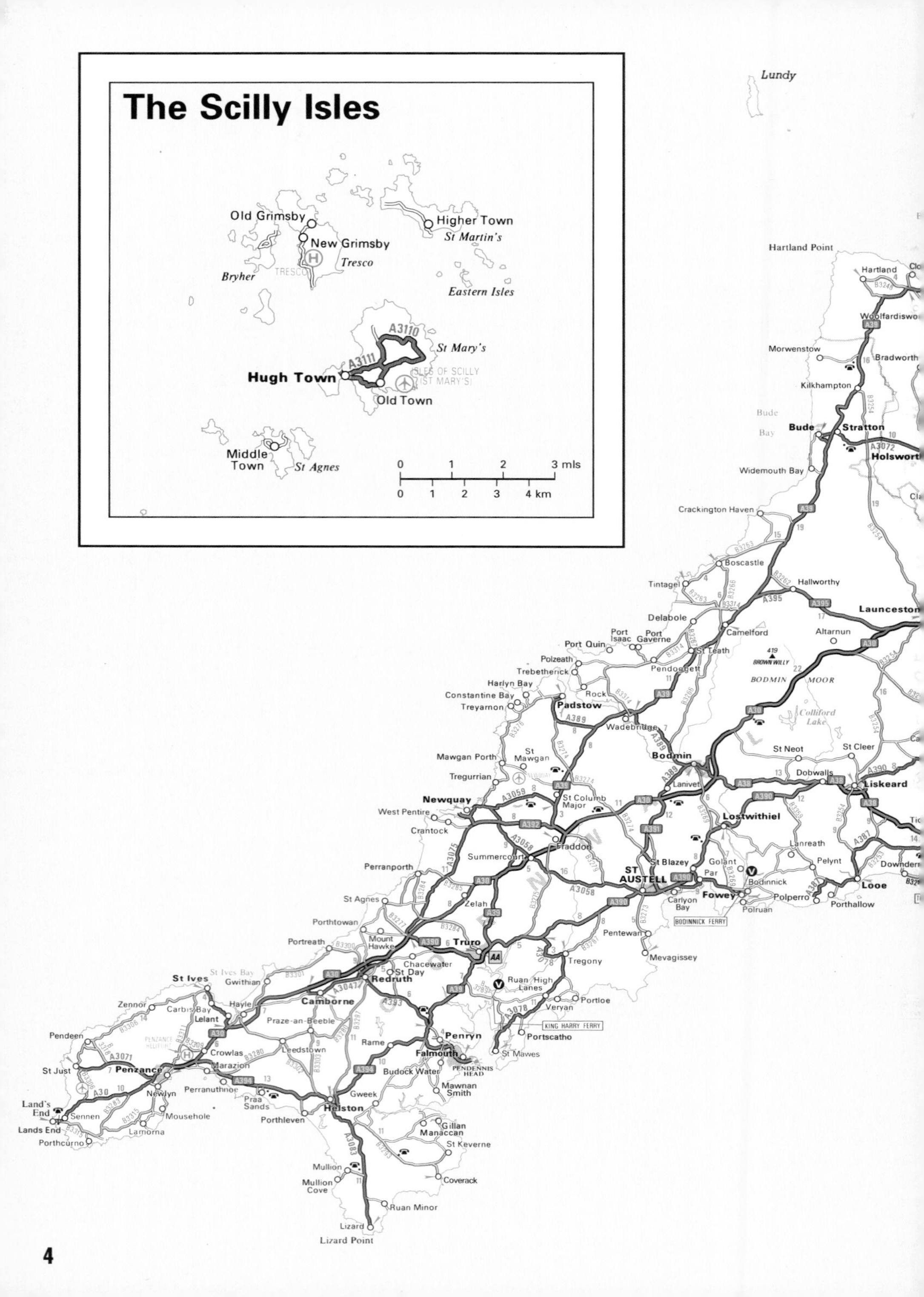

The Scilly Isles
Old Grimsby
New Grimsby
Higher Town
St Martin's
Tresco
Bryher
Eastern Isles
St Mary's
Hugh Town
Old Town
Middle Town
St Agnes
0 1 2 3 mls
0 1 2 3 4 km
Lundy
Hartland Point
Hartland
Woolfardisworthy
Morwenstow
Bradworthy
Kilkhampton
Bude Bay
Bude
Stratton
Holsworthy
Widemouth Bay
Crackington Haven
Boscastle
Tintagel
Hallworthy
Launceston
Delabole
Camelford
Altarnun
Port Quin
Port Isaac
Port Gaverne
St Teath
Polzeath
Trebetherick
Pendoggett
Brown Willy
Bodmin Moor
Harlyn Bay
Constantine Bay
Treyarnon
Rock
Padstow
Wadebridge
Colliford Lake
Mawgan Porth
St Mawgan
Bodmin
St Neot
St Cleer
Tregurrian
Dobwalls
Liskeard
Newquay
Lanivet
St Columb Major
West Pentire
Crantock
Lostwithiel
Fraddon
Summercourt
Lanreath
Pelynt
Perranporth
St Blazey
Golant
St Austell
Par
Bodinnick
Fowey
Polperro
Looe
Porthallow
St Agnes
Zelah
Carlyon Bay
Polruan
Bodinnick Ferry
Porthtowan
Pentewan
Portreath
Mount Hawke
Truro
Tregony
Mevagissey
Chacewater
St Day
Redruth
St Ives
St Ives Bay
Gwithian
Camborne
Ruan High Lanes
Portloe
Zennor
Carbis Bay
Hayle
Lelant
Veryan
Praze-an-Beeble
King Harry Ferry
Pendeen
Penryn
Portscatho
Crowlas
Leedstown
Rame
Marazion
Falmouth
St Mawes
St Just
Penzance
Pendennis Head
Budock Water
Newlyn
Perranuthnoe
Praa Sands
Mawnan Smith
Gweek
Land's End
Sennen
Mousehole
Helston
Lands End
Porthleven
Gillan
Manaccan
Lamorna
St Keverne
Porthcurno
Mullion
Coverack
Mullion Cove
Ruan Minor
Lizard
Lizard Point

Brean
Lympsham
Sedgemoor
Bridgwater
Bay
Berrow
Burnham-on-Sea
Highbridge
Woody
Bay
Lynton
Lynmouth
Porlock
Weir
Porlock
Minehead
Ilfracombe
Martinhoe
Combe
Martin
Brendon
Mortehoe
Lee
Berrynarbor
Dunster
Blue
Anchor
Watchet
Kilve
Stogursey
Woolacombe
EXMOOR
EXMOOR FOREST
DUNKERY
BEACON
Wheddon
Cross
Bilbrook
Williton
West
Quantoxhead
Holford
Croyde
Bratton
Fleming
Simonsbath
Exford
NATIONAL
PARK
Nether
Stowey
Muddiford
Braunton
BRENDON
HILLS
QUANTOCK HILLS
Saunton
Withypool
Winsford
BRIDGWATER
Yelland
Barnstaple
Brayford
North Petherton
Appledore
Northam
Instow
Bishop's
Tawton
North Molton
Wimbleball
Lake
Bishops
Lydeard
Othery
Ward Ho!
Bideford
South
Molton
Dulverton
Wiveliscombe
Langport
Landcross
Umberleigh
Exebridge
TAUNTON
Monkleigh
Bampton
Wellington
Hatch
Beauchamp
Parkham
Chittlehamholt
Taunton
Deane
Torrington
Burlescombe
MONUMENT
South
Petherton
Burrington
Culmstock
Horton
Chulmleigh
Witheridge
Withleigh
Sampford
Peverell
Hemyock
Ilminster
Chawleigh
Tiverton
Uffculme
Eggesford
Lapford
Yarcombe
Crewkerne
Chard
Black
Torrington
Winkleigh
Cheriton
Fitzpaine
Bickleigh
Cullompton
Upottery
Highampton
Hatherleigh
Chardstock
Membury
North
Tawton
Copplestone
Broadwindsor
Thorverton
Hawkchurch
Fenny
Bridges
Wilmington
Crediton
Stoke
Canon
Honiton
Axminster
Newton
St Cyres
Whimple
Gittisham
Okehampton
Tedburn
St Mary
EXETER
Ottery
St Mary
Musbury
Charmouth
Bratton Clovelly
Whiddon
Down
Clyst Honiton
Colyton
Roadford
Reservoir
South Zeal
Crockernwell
Cheriton
Bishop
Lyme
Regis
Sourton
Throwleigh
Longdown
Rousdon
621
HIGH WILLHAYS
Newton
Poppleford
Beer
Seaton
Lewdown
Chagford
Topsham
Branscombe
DARTMOOR
Sidmouth
Lyme Bay
Lydford
Moretonhampstead
Kennford
Lifton
Starcross
Budleigh
Salterton
DARTMOOR
FOREST
EXMOUTH
Mary Tavy
Bovey
Tracey
Chudleigh
Widecombe-
in-the-Moor
Haytor
Vale
Ideford
Ilsington
Two
Bridges
NATIONAL
Dawlish
Chudleigh
Knighton
Tavistock
Bishopsteignton
Teignmouth
Kingsteignton
Gunnislake
Princetown
Shaldon
Gulworthy
Hexworthy
Poundsgate
Combeinteignhead
Horrabridge
Newton
Abbot
Holne
PARK
Ashburton
Kingskerswell
Maidencombe
Yelverton
St Marychurch
Ipplepen
Bere
Alston
Buckfastleigh
Babbacombe
Bere
Ferrers
Staverton
TORQUAY
Marldon
TAMAR BR
(TOLL)
South
Brent
PAIGNTON
Cornwood
Tor Bay
Saltash
Wrangaton
Totnes
Ivybridge
Stoke Gabriel
Churston
Ferrers
Plympton
Brixham
Torpoint
PLYMOUTH
Ermington
Halwell
Yealmpton
Kingswear
Millbrook
Modbury
Dartmouth
Down
Thomas
Holbeton
DARTMOUTH FERRIES
Wembury
Newton
Ferrers
Strete
Stoke
Fleming
Bigbury-on-Sea
Slapton
Bigbury
Bay
Kingsbridge
Thurlestone
Chillington
Start Bay
South Milton
Hope
Malborough
Torcross
SANTANDER
Summer Only
ROSCOFF
Salcombe
East
Portlemouth
Start Point
0
10 miles
0
10 kilometres

DEVON

Appledore
Small town on A386, 3 miles (5km) N of Bideford

Appledore stands at the junction of the big estuaries of the Taw and Torridge; narrow streets packed with plain whitewashed cottages run up a gentle hill and along the estuary. There are shipyards along the Torridge River, with Braunton Burrows sand dunes further up the coast and a hilly landscape inland. The North Devon Maritime Museum is located here.

North Devon Maritime Museum
Odun House, Odun Road
Tel: 01237 474852

Appledore's traditional activities of boat-building and fishing make the village a suitable home for the museum. Each room shows a different aspect of North Devon's maritime history, including steam and motor coasters. There is also a full-size reconstruction of an Appledore kitchen of around 1900. A Victorian schoolroom, recreating an Appledore schoolroom c1890-1900, is available (with costumes) for school parties.

Open Etr–Oct, daily.

Devon's maritime traditions are celebrated at the museum

Arlington Court
(7 miles NE of Barnstaple, on A39)
Tel: 01271 850296

Built in 1822, Arlington Court, near the tiny hamlet of Arlington, is filled with a fascinating collection of *objets d'art*: pewter, shells and model ships as well as furniture and costumes from the 19th century. The biggest attraction, however, is the collection of carriages and horse-drawn vehicles, and rides are available. Around the house is a landscaped park grazed by Shetland ponies and sheep. There is a

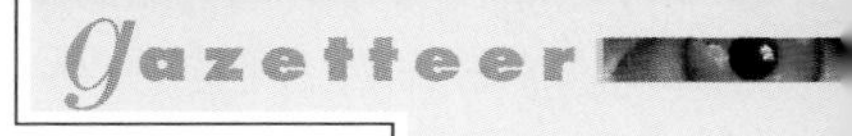

Victorian garden and a conservatory, and nature trails may be followed through the woods and by the lake.

Open Apr–Oct, Sun–Fri; also Sat of BH wknds. Footpaths through park open all year during daylight hours.

BARNSTAPLE
TOWN ON A39, 9 MILES (14KM) NE OF BIDEFORD

Barnstaple was the largest port on the North Devon coast until the 18th century. (See also page 50.)

BICKLEIGH
VILLAGE ON A396, 4 MILES (6KM) S OF TIVERTON

Bickleigh lies across the Exe Valley, with thatched cottages and a 16th-century bridge making a pretty picture. The castle stands in an idyllic setting by the river. The mill has crafts, rural displays and animals.

Bickleigh Castle
(OFF A396, FOLLOW SIGNS FROM BICKLEIGH BRIDGE)
TEL: 01884 855363

The 'castle' is really a moated and fortified manor house, and was formerly the romantic home of the heirs of the Earls of Devon and later of the Carew family. The small detached thatched chapel is said to be the oldest complete building in Devon. It dates from the Norman period and, like the medieval Gatehouse, survived the destruction which followed the Civil War. The Carew family acquired the house in the 16th century, and it was Admiral Sir George Carew who commanded the *Mary Rose* on her first and last voyage. He drowned with his men when the ship capsized and sank. There is an exhibition on the ship and on Tudor maritime history, with a feature on the *Titanic* and model ships of bygone days. Also in the house is a museum of domestic objects and toys dating from the 18th century, and a display of gadgets used by World War II spies and POWs – one of the most complete collections known. More traditional features of interest include the Great Hall, armoury (including fine Civil War armour), guardroom, Elizabethan bedroom and the 17th-century farmhouse. The garden is moated and the tower can be climbed for views of the Exe Valley and of the castle complex.

Open Etr wk (Good Fri–Fri), then Wed, Sun and BH to late May BH, then daily (except Sat) to Oct.

BIDEFORD
TOWN OFF A39, 9 MILES (14KM) SW OF BARNSTAPLE

This town on the estuary of the River Torridge was a successful port from the late 17th century. There are fine 17th- and 18th-century merchants' houses in Bridgeland Street, but the general appearance of the town is now rather neglected. The large covered market dates from 1883, from where narrow twisting streets lead up the hill.

The long bridge dates from the 13th century, but has been extensively repaired.

Other attractions of the town include the Burton Gallery and a museum of local interest.

BRIXHAM
TOWN ON A3022, 5 MILES (8KM) S OF PAIGNTON

The Great Western Railway arrived in Brixham in 1868, giving the local fishing industry an instant boost as London was now only seven hours away. The industry flourished into the 20th century, but by 1939 a mere half dozen boats were left. Following a revival in the 1960s, a new fish market and a deep water jetty complete with its own ice-making plant were opened in 1971

Torbay, on 'the English Riviera', is one of the West Country's leading tourist honeypots. At the southern end of the bay the picturesque harbour and the steep, narrow streets of Brixham lie sheltered in the lee of Berry Head. In 1850 the town claimed to be England's leading fishing port, with more than 270 vessels – brigs, schooners and smacks – amounting to 20,000 tons of shipping. The town still has a fishing fleet, but a much smaller one. At the harbour's edge a statue of William of Orange commemorates his arrival here in 1688 on his way to be proclaimed King William III at Newton Abbot – and later in London. Near by, a full-size replica of Sir Francis Drake's *Golden Hind*, the ship in which he sailed round the world, is moored close to the old market house. The local history is expounded in Brixham Museum, which has a special section on the coastguard service. Rev Henry Francis Lyte, who took charge of All Saints' Church in 1824, wrote the familiar hymn 'Abide With Me' in Brixham. A monument in the churchyard recalls 100 sailors who drowned in a terrible storm in 1866, when many boats were driven onto the rocks. The town's more modern Roman Catholic church has the curious and possibly unique distinction of having a car park located on its roof.

BUCKFAST
VILLAGE OFF A38, 1 MILE (1.5KM) N OF BUCKFASTLEIGH

Buckfast is situated in the Dart Valley just off Dartmoor. In medieval times there was a large monastery, abolished with all the others in the 1530s. In 1882 French Benedictines acquired the site and set out to rebuild it, finishing the buildings in 1938. Today there is a large church, and still a working monastery.

BUCKFASTLEIGH
TOWN OFF A38, 5 MILES (8KM) NW OF TOTNES

An early industrial centre, particularly for the manufacture of woollen cloth, with several mills surviving. Local attractions include Buckfast Butterfly Farm and Dartmoor Otter Sanctuary, and the Primrose Line, the Dart Valley Light Railway (steam) which runs to Totnes.

Buckfast Butterfly Farm and Dartmoor Otter Sanctuary
(OFF A38, AT DART BRIDGE JUNCT)
TEL: 01364 642916

Visitors can wander around a specially designed, undercover tropical garden, where free-flying butterflies and moths from around the world can be seen. The otter sanctuary has four large enclosures with underwater viewing areas. There are special viewing holts where sleeping otters may be observed.

Open daily, Etr–Oct.

Buckfast Abbey
TEL: 01364 642519

The story of Buckfast Abbey is a remarkable one. The monastery was originally founded in 1018, but the monks left during the Dissolution in the 16th century. Monks returned to the site in 1882 and considered restoring it; in 1907 four (mostly inexperienced) monks began rebuilding the church; and now Buckfast Abbey is once again a

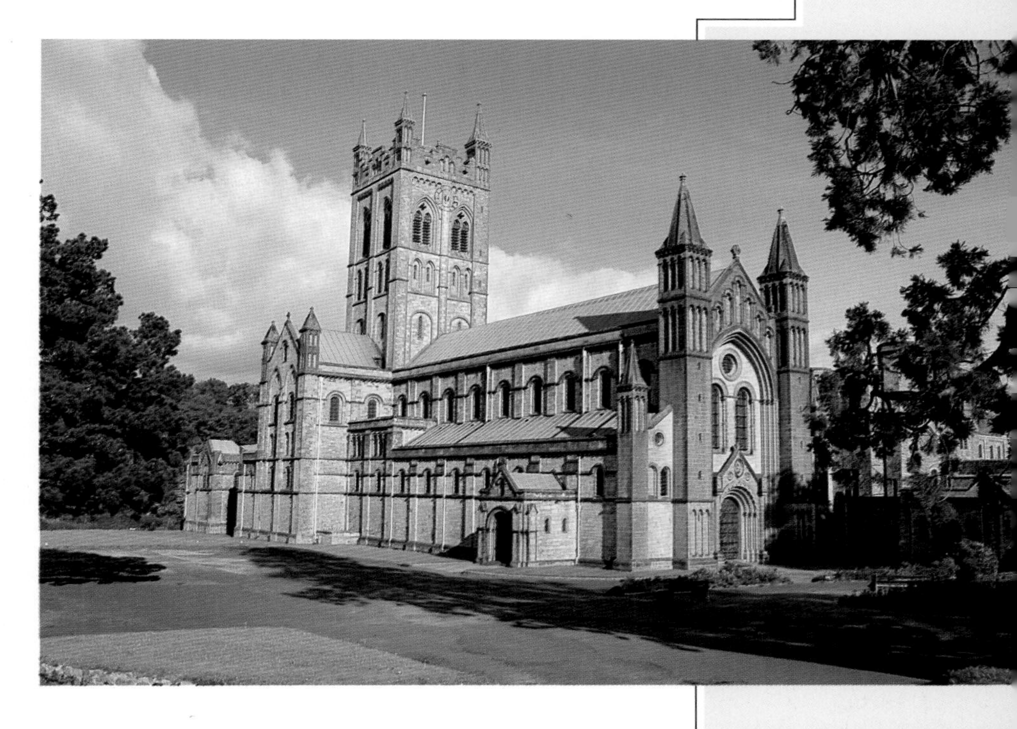

A visit to Buckfast Abbey provides an opportunity for quiet reflection

religious community. The church was built on the old foundations, using local blue limestone and Ham Hill stone. One of the most beautiful features is the great modern east window, which was the work of Father Charles, a craftsman in stained glass. Other monks have different skills: in beekeeping, farming, and the making of Buckfast tonic wine. In recent years restoration work has continued in the precinct, where several medieval monastic buildings survive including the 14th-century guest hall, which is open to the public and contains an exhibition of the history of the Abbey. Monthly concerts are held at the Abbey, please telephone for details.

Open all year daily; exhibition Etr–Oct.

CHULMLEIGH

Small town on B3096, 8 miles (13km) S of South Molton

Chulmleigh is a good example of the effects of changing transportation systems. The village grew up at the junction of five ancient roads and developed as an important market centre in what was, even before Domesday, a prosperous sheep-farming area. Its 15th-century church is a proud reminder of those days, its granite tower visible for miles around. Inside is an excellent, wide rood screen and a wagon roof with good bosses and ribs supported by the outspread wings of 38 carved angels. In 1830 a new turnpike from Exeter to Barnstaple bypassed the town and in 1854 the railway came and markets moved to stations.

The Barnstaple Inn, dated 1633 but possibly of earlier origin.was used as a courthouse and had a gibbet over the door for the execution of offenders.

Even before then, competition from the North had dealt a blow to the woollen trade, and soon improvements in farming practices led to further unemployment. Add to this two disastrous fires in the 19th century, and Chulmleigh's days of prosperity were numbered. Some wonderful old merchants' houses, many cob, stone and thatched cottages, as well as a medieval toll-house, have survived.

CLOVELLY

Village off A39, 9 miles (14km) W of Bideford

Tumbling like a foaming cataract down the North Devon cliff, the white-washed houses of this famously picturesque village seem to stand almost on top of each other. The 400-ft (122-m) main street, which is cobbled with stones from the beach below, falls sharply down steps and is far too steep for cars. Donkeys used to carry visitors up and down, but nowadays you walk down on your own two feet, past cottages bright with fuchsias and nasturtiums in window boxes and hanging baskets (behind the Red Lion Inn a Land Rover lurks to take the leg-weary back to the top). At the bottom is the sturdy stone quay, where fishing boats shelter in the harbour by the former lifeboat house. The quay was built by one of the Cary squires in the 16th century and extended in the 1820s. With one of the few safe harbours on this rock-ribbed coast, Clovelly lived principally by fishing until tourism overtook it as a more profitable source of income. A visitor centre at the car park tells the story of the village's colourful past. Its old-world charm has been preserved by strong-minded squires, notably Mrs Christine Hamlyn, a formidable lady who inherited Clovelly and made

Westward Ho!
Clovelly's fine quay was built by George Cary, the 16th-century squire whose son William plays a prominent and dashing role in Charles Kingsley's Westward Ho! *(1855). It was this popular historical novel that first marked Clovelly as a tourist attraction. Kingsley knew the village well – his father was Rector of Clovelly in the 1830s and Charles spent part of his boyhood at the rectory. Both* Westward Ho! *and* The Water Babies *were written here.*

A steep climb leads to Clovelly's tiny harbour

her husband take her surname instead of the customary way round. Tiny and iron-willed, she ruled the village with a passionate and tyrannical affection for 50 years from 1884 until her death in the 1930s, and the initials CH on many of the buildings are hers. It was she who insisted on barring the motor car, and to this day all vehicles have to be left at the top of the village.

The most attractive approach to Clovelly was constructed by one of her ancestors, Sir James Hamlyn Williams, between 1811 and 1829, partly to provide work for Clovelly men after the Napoleonic Wars. This is the Hobby Drive, which opens off the A39 west of Bideford and makes its winding way for three miles down the cliffs through delectable woods with stunning vistas over Bideford Bay. Monuments of generations of the Carys, Hamlyns and Fanes stud the walls of the simple medieval parish church of All Saints, with its 17th-century pews, pulpit and hour-glass. Some of the pillars are of granite brought from Lundy Island, some 12 miles (19km) out in the Bristol Channel. Up in the hamlet of Higher Clovelly, on private land, are the remains of an Iron Age hill fort, which was apparently designed specially for herding cattle, perhaps gathered here for export abroad. Now, not far away, you can watch today's cows being milked at a working dairy farm called the Milky Way.

'The Three Fishers'
Three fishers went sailing away to the west,
Away to the west as the sun went down;
Each thought on the woman who loved him the best
And the children stood watching them out of the town.
CHARLES KINGSLEY

COCKINGTON

1½ MILES (2.5KM) W OF TORQUAY

It is not often one can say that a village's recent history may be as significant as its past. During World War II the Prudential Building Society evacuated its staff to Torquay, and a rapport built up with the locals so that, when the privately owned Cockington Estate was about to be split up, the Prudential decided to invest in its thatched cottages and shops *en bloc*, maintaining them in traditional style and thus preserving on the outskirts of Torquay this quaint Domesday village.

Some of the cottages have Saxon origins and the 13th- and 14th-century red sandstone church has Norman foundations. The old forge dates from the 14th century. The only modern building is the thatched Drum Inn, built in harmonious style by Sir Edwin Lutyens in 1934. Cockington Court, the Elizabethan manor of the Carys and then of the Mallocks who added its façade, is owned by Torbay Borough Council and is now home to the Devon Rural Skills Trust who provide workspace for such threatened craftsworkers as the blacksmith, hurdlemaker and thatcher. Its grounds are a designated country park, open to all. For decades now horse-drawn carriages have brought visitors out here from Torquay seafront. These visitors have inevitably caused the appearance of litter bins and public conveniences, but tourism has had a positive effect in that the village's immediate environment has developed naturally and unobtrusively.

This ride takes you through fine Devon countryside and along the River Exe. It uses, in the main, quiet undulating lanes with no off-road cycling, but for a busier scene, there are opportunities to stop at the seaside resorts of Dawlish Warren and Dawlish.

INFORMATION

Total Distance:
18 miles (29km)

Grade:
2

OS Map:
Landranger 1:50,000 sheet 192 (Exeter & Sidmouth)

Tourist Information:
Exeter. Tel: 01392 265700

Cycle Shops/Hire:
Richard's Bikes, Exeter, tel: 01392 79688; Saddles and Paddles, Exeter, tel: 01392 424241

Nearest railway station:
Exeter St Davids (2½ miles/4km)

Refreshments:
Pubs in Exminster include The Stowey Arms, and The Turf by the river; also Drons Lodge at Dawlish Warren, and Bow Windows at Dawlish

The imposing pumping station designed by Brunel

START

Exminster is just off the Matford roundabout on the A379, and not far from junction 30 of the M5. The ride starts from the car parking area in the centre of town, where there are a public telephone box and toilets.

DIRECTIONS

1. Turn left from the car park to head down to Exminster Hill, where a right turn by Exminster Chapel brings the first steep hill. Continue to the top and, ignoring the right turn to Soloman Farm, carry straight on down past Crablake Farm, for 1 mile (1.5km) to reach the junction with the A379. Cross the A379 with care to Red Lodge, signposted 'Powderham'. Down this road, to your left, there are good views of a round house, the river and the ship canal. Topsham and Exton can be seen across the river. Continue straight on towards Powderham. Pass the Castle Tower on your right, and follow the road past the gates of Powderham Castle Estate. Bear left towards St Clement's Church at the bottom of the avenue of trees and follow the road sharp right around the church.

2. Continue on this road between the railway and the estate, where you may catch a glimpse of the deer herd. Pass the Starcross Sailing Club on the left, with good views of Lympstone and Exmouth across the river, and reach a junction with the A379. Bear left here, towards Starcross. Just past the public toilets, look out for a red sandstone tower on the left of the road: this is Brunel's Pumping House. Stay on the A379 to Cockwood Harbour, and turn left towards Dawlish Warren.

The estuary of the River Exe is a popular sailing area

3. Ignore right turns and proceed along the riverside to a T-junction, just past Dawlish Sands Holiday Camp. Turn right to pass Drons Lodge, and go up a short, steep rise. Continue, past The Mount

Pleasant Inn and the Langstone Cliff Hotel, towards Dawlish, to turn left at the T-junction, back onto the A379. Cycling parallel to the sea front, enter a traffic calming area. Pass a church on the right and on descending a hill, bear left, following the road to the sea front. Keep on this road around a stream area, and bear right and left to go upstream. Pass a large water-wheel on the left and proceed to the T-junction, at end of Brunswick Place. Turn right and bear right, to turn left up Queen Street. Follow the road around to the left on Park Road, passing the RAFA and British Legion Clubs on the right. Continue into Old Town Street, and on to narrow blind corner. Turn right with care, passing The Swan Inn, and bear left towards Ashcombe.

4. At a T-junction turn right up an extremely steep but short hill and bear left to follow beside Dawlish Water for nearly 2 miles (3km). Ignore the right turn by nursery greenhouses, but take the next right, signposted to Starcross, up a narrow rise. At the top, to the left is a view of the Haldon Obelisk. Descend with care, heading straight across a five-point junction, down a long hill. Bear left at the bottom to pass Gulliford House and reach the 'Basket Lodge' signpost. Continue straight on, signposted 'Starcross'. Ignore all turnings until you reach the Black Forest Lodge, after about 1½ miles (2.5km).

5. Cross straight over this junction, but take great care, as the left side is blind. Proceed straight on, crossing Haydon Common, past Willsworthy Farm, and on to Willsworthy Cross crossroads. At this junction proceed straight ahead up the hill and at the next junction, turn right towards Exminster. Follow this lane to a T-junction. Turn left here, down a steep hill into the village; turn left at the T-junction at the bottom of the hill, and retrace your route to the car park.

PLACES OF INTEREST

Exminster

Set on the west bank of the River Exe, Exminster has become a peaceful, pleasant backwater of a town since the building of a by-pass. The church dates back as far as the 8th century and has a notable set of bells, as well as some exceptionally fine plasterwork dating from 1633.

Powderham Castle

The home of the Earl of Devon is a medieval fortified manor house, extended and altered in the 18th and 19th centuries, but with a core some 400 years older, commanding wonderful views over the estate to the river. Flamboyantly decorated rooms

WHAT TO LOOK OUT FOR

The stone pillar of Haldon Obelisk was erected as a beacon to assist sailors, and is set in a delightfully wooded area of the Haldon Hills.

are beautifully furnished, and the castle is well worth a visit (open from the end of March to early October). The extensive grounds are home to a large herd of fallow deer, and these can often be glimpsed from the road to Starcross through Powderham.

Starcross

Isambard Kingdom Brunel, the great Victorian engineer, had much to do with the development of the south-west, thanks to his involvement in the Great Western Railway system. The strange red-brick Pumping Tower in Starcross is about all that remains of his experimental 'atmospheric railway', by which trains were running at up to 70mph (113kph) as early as 1818. During the summer months, a ferry plies between Starcross and Exmouth.

Rails, sand and sea, make for a sea front with a difference at Dawlish

Dawlish

This quaint holiday town is a pleasant place to explore, with the Dawlish Water stream running through the centre. This provides a haven of peace where the famous Dawlish black swans can be fed by visitors.

COMBE MARTIN
Small town on A399, 4 miles (6km) E of Ilfracombe

Combe Martin consists of one very long street running down a shallow valley, with a pretty bay at the end. There is a fine rocky coast, especially eastwards to Hangman Point. The church is 15th-century, built in red sandstone, with good wooden screens. Holdstone Down to the east gives panoramic views. Attractions include Combe Martin Wildlife and Dinosaur Park, Farm World at Berry Down, Combe Martin Motor Cycle Collection and a museum.

Bodstone Barton Farmworld & Playland
Berrydown, 2 miles (3km) S of Combe Martin, off A3123
Tel: 01271 883654

Set in an area of outstanding natural beauty, Bodstone Barton is a 17th-century farm covering 160 acres (65ha). The farm is run by both traditional and modern methods, and visitors can see goats being milked by hand. Attractions include an adventure playground, and rides by tractor, trailer and horse-drawn cart. There is a nature trail to follow, with an abundance of wildlife to be seen. A collection of agricultural and domestic items are on show, with 20,000 square feet (1858sq m) under cover. Visitors can watch heavy horses being groomed and harnessed. There are plenty of rides, and a large undercover children's area – 'Playland'.

Open all year, daily.

The Combe Martin Motor Cycle Collection
Cross St (adjacent to the main car park, behind beach)
Tel: 01271 882346

The collection was formed in 1979 and contains old and new British motorcycles, displayed against a background of old petrol pumps, signs and garage equipment, exhibiting motoring nostalgia in an old-world atmosphere.

Open Etr then May–Nov, daily.

Lovingly preserved exhibits at the Motorcycle Collection

Combe Martin Wildlife Park & Dinosaur Park
Tel: 01271 882486

Twenty acres (8ha) of woodland complete with streams, cascading waterfalls, ornamental gardens, tropical plants and rare trees make this perhaps the most natural wildlife park in Britain. Otters living in the streams have produced 29 young in the last five years, and for something completely different, visitors can see meerkats 'on guard', living in the largest enclosure in Europe – a man-made desert. There is also a large selection of primates, mammals and birds. The Domain of the Dinosaurs has partially animated life-size dinosaurs set in prehistoric woodland.

Open Etr–Oct, daily.

DARTINGTON
VILLAGE ON A384, 2 MILES (3KM) NW OF TOTNES

Dartington Hall (limited opening) is famous for its medieval architecture, for music and for glass. The 14th-century hall makes one side of a fine court of buildings. The gardens are worth a visit, and the Dartington Cider Press Centre is housed in 16th- and 17th-century stone buildings.

DARTMOUTH
TOWN ON A379, 7 MILES (11KM) SE OF TOTNES

Dartmouth is an ancient port, sheltering inside the mouth of the Dart estuary, and built up a steep hillside. Houses line the riverside, and the town has a charming mixture of buildings, some timber-framed. The 17th-century Butterwalk (with the museum) is particularly fine. Two ferries (one for vehicles) operate across the river to Kingswear, and another a little north on the main road, by the huge late-Victorian Royal Naval College. Dartmouth Castle (English Heritage) is on the rocks at the river entrance, dates from the 1480s, and stands next to a large church dating from 1642.

Dartmouth Castle
TEL: 01803 833588

At the mouth of the River Dart a rocky promontory juts out towards the sea, and on this rock stands Dartmouth Castle – an intriguing collection of military buildings spanning six centuries. The most recent addition is a brick gun-shelter built during World War II in anticipation of a German invasion.

A castle was built at Dartmouth in the 14th century, although it was not until the 15th century that the citizens of Dartmouth really began to build their fortress in earnest. It comprised a square tower and a round tower, side by side, moulded to suit the shape of the rock, and is the earliest surviving English coastal castle designed specially for artillery. At the same time, another castle was built opposite Dartmouth at Kingswear, ensuring that no French pirates would be able to penetrate up river to pillage the wealthy town. A chain could be drawn between the two in times of war, and the timber-framed opening for the chain can still be seen.

The castle itself saw action in the Civil War, when the town was attacked by Cromwell's forces under Sir Thomas Fairfax. In a blaze of gunfire, Fairfax's men stormed the town, taking it within hours and with remarkably few casualties. The 500 Royalists, who had captured Dartmouth Castle after a siege three years before, surrendered their arms on the following day.

Open all year. Closed 24–26 Dec and 1 Jan.

Bayard's Cove Fort
(ON RIVERFRONT)

The low, circular ruined stronghold was built by the townspeople to protect the harbour. It stands at the southern end of the cove, where the cobbled quay was used as a location for 'The Onedin Line'.

Open at all reasonable times.

Dartmouth Museum
6 Butterwalk
Tel: 01803 832923

The timber-framed 17th-century house is part of a restored colonnaded arcade, and is encrusted with carvings. It houses a small maritime museum with over 150 ship models and many pictures and artefacts relating to the history of this ancient town.

Open all year, Mon–Sat at certain times.

Newcomen Memorial Engine
The Engine House, Mayors Av
Tel: 01803 834224 & 834959

Thomas Newcomen helped to keep open Devon's mines by inventing a steam-driven pump to clear them of water. This building was erected to commemorate the 300th anniversary of his birth (1663) and houses one of his atmospheric pumping engines of 1725.

Open all year, certain days.

Woodland Leisure Park
Blackawton (W, off A3122)
Tel: 01803 712598

A beautiful 60-acre (24-ha) park with indoor and outdoor attractions for all the family. There are 12 playzones including a commando course, the 500m Tornado Toboggan Run, action tracks, amazing matrix and a special toddlers' play village, also a vast under cover play area. The Circus Playdrome offers bouncy castles, dressing up in circus costumes, crazy bikes and a circus ring. The large animal complex and wildlife walkabout has hundreds of animals and birds, and there is an international wildfowl collection and Bee Observatory. Live entertainment days all through the school holidays.

Open all year, daily .

DAWLISH
Town on A379, 12 miles (19km) S of Exeter

This early seaside resort features a group of 19th-century villas surrounding the 'Lawn'.

(See also page 15.)

EXETER
City off M5, 64 miles (103km) SW of Bristol

Historically and psychologically the capital of the south-west, this cathedral city is a county town, a university town and a major focus of road and rail routes. Although severely damaged in World War II, it has retained much of its history and charm. The city stands on the site of a Roman fort on a hill above the River Exe. Stretches of the Roman wall have been kept in good repair.

The cathedral boasts two massive Norman towers and 300ft (91m) of the longest unbroken stretch of tierceron vaulting in the world. Standing beneath it in the nave has been compared to being inside a whale. There is also an elaborate medieval clock, the first English attempt to depict an elephant, and delightful carvings done when bomb damage was repaired after 1945 – among them the one-eyed cathedral cat. The cathedral library contains the fabled *Exeter Book*, the premier manuscript of Anglo-Saxon poetry.

Little city churches in the local crumbly red sandstone were fitted into bustling medieval Exeter at odd angles. The guildhall is one of Britain's oldest municipal buildings and the Ship Inn was Sir Francis Drake's favourite hostelry. The Royal Albert Memorial Museum and Art Gallery is in a fine Victorian building, and part of the medieval St Nicholas Priory can be visited. Guided tours through the Underground Passages, which brought water to the medieval city, are irresistible except for the claustrophobic; the entrance is in the Princesshay shopping precinct. Today a premier administrative, financial and business centre, Exeter prides itself on excellent shopping and attractive gardens.

Guildhall
HIGH ST
TEL: 01392 77888

This is one of the oldest municipal buildings still in use. It was built in 1330 and then altered in 1446, and the arches and façade were added in 1592-5. The roof timbers rest on bosses depicting bears holding staves, and there are portraits of Exeter dignitaries, guild crests, civic silver and regalia.

Open when there are no mayoral functions. Times are posted outside weekly. Special opening by arrangement.

Royal Albert Memorial Museum
QUEEN ST
TEL: 01392 265858

Founded in 1865, the museum is especially interesting for Exeter silver, regional archaeology and Devon paintings. Other displays include a traditional natural history display, a Victorian collection of shells, and beautiful African wood carvings. There is a temporary exhibition programme and children's activities are held during school holidays.

Open all year, Mon–Sat.

Exeter's Cathedral Close

St Nicholas' Priory
MINT LANE, OFF FORE ST
TEL: 01392 265858

The Benedictine priory was founded in 1070, and its remains include unusual survivals such as the Norman undercroft, a Tudor room and a 15th-century kitchen. Some fine plaster decoration can be seen, and there are displays of furniture and wood carving. There is a programme of temporary exhibitions.

Open Etr–Oct, Mon–Sat.

Underground Passages
BOOTS ARCADE, HIGH ST
TEL: 01392 265858

A unique medieval water system with an introductory exhibition. This is definitely not suitable for those inclined to claustrophobia. These are the only ancient city passageways open to the public. All tours are guided and there is an introductory 10-minute videoplus exhibition. Flat shoes are essential.

Open Jul–Sep and school holidays, Mon–Sat; rest of year Tue–Sat.

EXMOOR
SCENIC AREA IN SW ENGLAND

Exmoor, sometimes seen as the poor relation to Dartmoor, has its own strong character and particular scenery. It is a high moorland plateau in northern Devon and Somerset (mainly Somerset) bordering the Bristol Channel. The national park of 265 square miles (685sq km), designated in 1954, includes the Brendon Hills, in a landscape which blends moor and heath with farms and swift streams in deep, lushly wooded valleys, and England's highest sea cliffs on the Bristol Channel coast.

Once all wild hunting country, Exmoor was partly tamed in the 19th

From Dunkery Beacon views extend over the Bristol Channel to the Welsh coast

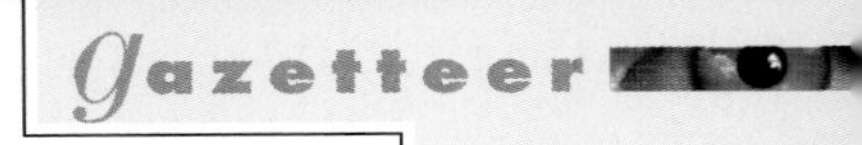

century by a rich ironmaster, John Knight, who turned 15,000 acres (6070ha) into farmland, planting miles of beech hedges which still survive. Today there are many enjoyable walking routes, prehistoric sites, ancient packhorse bridges and whortleberry bushes, with red deer and wild ponies, although the pony population is declining.

The highest point is Dunkery Beacon at 1,705ft (502m), commanding huge views, in an extensive National Trust estate. The valleys of the Barle, the Exe and the twin Lyn rivers are especially lovely. Romantic associations with R D Blackmore's *Lorna Doone* draw visitors to Badgeworthy Water and the Doone Valley, and the diminutive church at Oare, where Lorna Doone and John Rigg were married.

GREAT TORRINGTON
TOWN ON A386, 5 MILES (8KM) SE OF BIDEFORD

This market town is dramatically sited, with a steep cliff overlooking the River Torridge. The classical town hall and a pannier market are found in the dense centre, where there is also a small museum. In the lower part is Dartington Crystal, with displays of glass-making. Rosemoor Garden, 1 mile (1.5km) south-east, is being expanded by the Royal Horticultural Society to include rose, bog and many other gardens. The Great Torrington Steam Railway is based here.

(See also 'A Picnic at The Old Bowling Green', page 22.)

Dartington Crystal
LINDEN CLOSE
TEL: 01805 624233 & 01805 623797

Tours of the factory are conducted from the safety of viewing galleries that overlook the craftsmen, who can be seen carrying out the age-old techniques of glass manufacture and processing; there are also studio glass-making demonstrations. The Visitor Centre has a permanent exhibition tracing the history of glass and crystal over the past 2,000 years. The factory shop sells slightly imperfect crystal.

Open all year. Factory & Visitor Centre: Mon–Fri. Shop & Restaurant: open daily. Closed 25–26 Dec & Etr Sun.

RHS Garden Rosemoor
TEL: 01805 624067

Started in 1959, Lady Anne's garden contains many rare plants. It is sheltered in a wooded valley and covers about 8 acres (3ha). There are species and hybrid rhododendrons, shrub roses and a wide variety of ornamental trees and shrubs. A new 32-acre (13-ha) garden is nearing completion. It already contains 2000 roses of 200 varieties, two large colour theme gardens, a herb garden and potager, an extensive herbaceous border, stream and bog gardens, a cottage garden, a foliage and plantsman's garden, and a fruit and vegetable garden.

Gardens open all year; Visitor Centre open certain times.

This popular but unspoiled picnic site on the outskirts of the hilltop town of Great Torrington, high above the River Torridge and with outstanding views of rolling countryside and wooded valley glades, is ideal for family picnics and lovely walks on the common land surrounding the town.

HOW TO GET THERE

Take the A386 out of Great Torrington and head towards Bideford. Just as you leave the town, the Old Bowling Green is on your right, before you descend the hill towards the Torridge Valley and the Old Torrington Railway Station; this is now a restaurant called 'The Puffing Billy'.

For the Tarka Trail site, continue on the A386 north-west for 2½ miles (4km), following the river.

FACILITIES

Hot and cold snacks are available all year from a kiosk.
There are numerous tables, and toilets near by.
Playground with swings.
Free parking.
Special dog owners' car park.
Dog owners are encouraged to exercise their pets on the lower part of the common and to keep the main picnic area a dog-free area.
Car boot sales every Sunday morning.

The Old Bowling Green is a large, sensitively developed hilltop picnic site beside the main road from Great Torrington to Bideford. Its slopes are contoured by many well-maintained paths, and a walk around the town lasts 1½ hours. The picnic site is popular throughout the year, especially on Sundays when, weather permitting, a car boot sale is held on the upper picnic area.

The Square in the market town of Great Torrington

Great Torrington

The Saxon market town of Great Torrington is well worth exploring, particularly around the square, with its antiquated Town Hall and

Market House. The town has a chequered history. During the Civil War it was the scene of fierce fighting; the church, used as a prison for Royalists captured by Roundheads, was also a gunpowder store until an explosion blew it to pieces, killing several hundred men. Today's church, built in 1651, contains an inscribed stone in memory of this tragic event, and the town museum documents how the Civil War affected the town. Opposite the church is Dartington Glassworks, Great Torrington's best-known industry. Just outside the town both Rosemoor Gardens, belonging to the Royal Horticultural Society, and the Barometer Museum at Merton are well worth a visit.

The Tarka Trail

This picnic is perfect for walkers, as Great Torrington is in the heart of Tarka country, with a 180-mile (290-km) walk based on Henry Williamson's book *Tarka the Otter*. Divided into sections and clearly signposted, it explores deepest Devon, covering much of the rocky North Devon coast, the Taw and Torridge rivers, Dartmoor and Exmoor, passing through the beautiful countryside so vividly described in the novel. However, do not expect to see otters because although they still inhabit the area, they are largely nocturnal creatures.

(See also Cycle Ride, The Tarka Trail, page 48.)

Black Torrington

This village, 5 miles (8km) west of Hatherleigh offf the A3072, was the last home of the Reverend John (Jack) Russell, who bred the terriers which bear his name, in the 19th century.

The Torrington Viaduct, on the Tarka Trail

A visually exciting walk from the dramatic headland of Hartland Quay to the quiet cove at Dyer's Lookout. The route then turns inland through woods and fields to Stoke village before returning to Hartland Quay.

Grid ref: SS226247

INFORMATION

The walk is 2½ miles (4km) long.
Mainly easy walking. There is a slight incline between Dyer's Lookout and Stoke.
Several stiles.
Dogs should be on leads at start of walk.
Good picnic area at Dyer's Lookout.
Cream teas at Stoke during the season.
Toilets at Stoke.
Hartland Quay Hotel serves bar meals; children welcome.
Small museum at Hartland Quay.

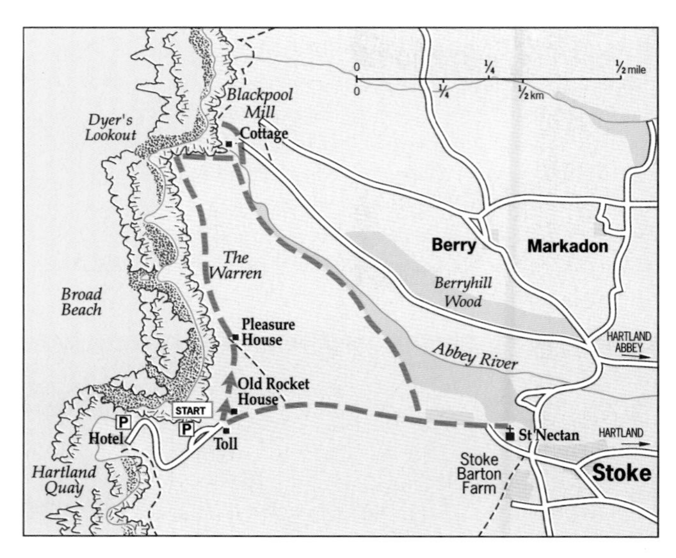

START

From the A39 turn onto the B3248, signed Hartland. Pass through the villages of Hartland and Stoke, following signs for Hartland Quay. There is a car park just inside the toll-gate and this makes a good starting point (other car parks lower down give easy access to the pub and museum).

DIRECTIONS

From the toll booth turn left, crossing a stile beside the Old Rocket House. Follow the coast path (keeping well in from the cliff edge) across open ground to pass a ruined building, keeping to the main footpath for approximately ¼ mile (0.5km). Where the path descends to Dyer's Lookout bear inland, following 'Coast Path' signs. Go through a gate. Turn left, cross over a stile and cross the Abbey River to gain the track that curves round to the left above an isolated cottage.

Go through a kissing-gate to reach a flat grassy area above the beach (there is a short stony descent to the beach to the right of an old bench looking seaward). Retrace your steps to cross the Abbey River. Turn inland along the public footpath and follow the tree-shaded path (can be muddy). Continue uphill alongside open fields. Just before the road turn sharp left over a stile and down a narrow path between hedges. Go through a gate and cross a stile, then go over another stile into the churchyard.

From the churchyard return to the field where the path from Dyer's joins from the north. Continue straight ahead along the left edge of the field to reach the car park.

Striking rock strata at Hartland Quay

Old Rocket House and the Pleasure House

The Old Rocket House was built in 1892 to house the wagon and rocket equipment of the newly formed Hartland Life Saving Apparatus Company. The team of life savers gave outstanding service to sailors in distress during many shipwrecks on this notorious stretch of scoast.

The roofless building just beyond the Rocket House is called the Pleasure House, believed to have been built as a summer house in the 18th century. The large archway is said to have been incorporated so that a coach could be backed inside. The cliff top between the Rocket House and Dyer's Lookout was a rabbit warren in the 19th century.

WHAT TO LOOK OUT FOR

There are many seabirds such as gannets, guillemots and fulmars, to be seen offshore. Kestrels may often be seen hovering just above the cliff edge, and peregrines are not uncommon. Dyer's Lookout is a good place to look out for grey seals. In clear weather you should be able to see the island of Lundy which lies about 10 miles (16km) north-north-west.

Church of St Nectan

The 128-ft (39-m) tower of this 14th-century church is one of the highest in Devon. St Nectan was a 5th-century Welsh saint and legend has it that one day, when he was out looking for his cattle, robbers attacked him and cut off his head. Undaunted, St Nectan tucked his head under his arm and walked the mile or so back to his holy well at Stoke, where he finally expired. The church and churchyard of St Nectan have many memorials to shipwrecked sailors. The western end of the graveyard is called Stranger's Hill and it is here that unidentified victims of shipwrecks lie buried.

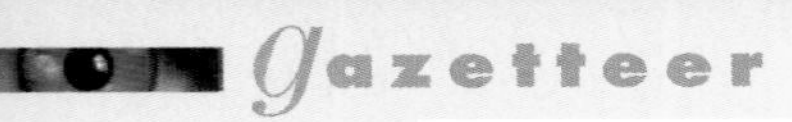

HARTLAND
Small town on B3248, 4 miles (6.5km) W of Clovelly

A town in medieval times, but never very successful because it was so remote, Hartland is now more like a village. The church is 2 miles (3km) away towards the sea, and is one of the finest in Devon, with a 130-ft (40-m) tower. The large and beautiful interior has fine wooden screens and roofs. Hartland Abbey (limited opening) is the big house, converted from monastic buildings, with attractive gardens.

HARTLAND POINT
Headland 3 miles (5km) NW of Hartland

The northernmost point of Devon has 350-ft (105-m) rocky cliffs, bleak and wild, and a big lighthouse to warn shipping. There is nothing between here and America. Hartland Quay is an area a little south of the Point, with particularly contorted geology and a museum. There are many coastal waterfalls here, and much of the coast is owned by the National Trust.

HEDDON'S MOUTH
Beauty spot off A39, 4 miles (6.5km) W of Lynton

Heddon's Mouth is the seaward end of a spectacularly steep valley reached via a footpath from the little woody hamlet of Hunter's Inn.

HEMERDON HOUSE
2 miles (3km) NE of Plympton
Tel: 01752 841410

Curiously, the man who built Hemerdon House had a father and father-in-law who shared the same name (Thomas Woollcombe) and the same occupation (surgeons) in the same town (Plymouth). The two were, in fact, related and young George and his wife Maria were cousins. It was Maria who brought the estate into the marriage and the house they built there was begun in 1793.

Delightfully unpretentious, the Georgian house is particularly interesting for the documentation of its occupation kept by successive generations of Woollcombes. Other momentoes of members of the family include the naval uniform and sword of George, son of the original owners, who rose to the rank of Vice Admiral and was wounded at the Battle of New Orleans. His brother, William, fought at Waterloo.

The present owner of Hemerdon, James Woollcombe, has undertaken much restoration in recent years, including the repairing and rebinding of the excellent collection of books in the library, which date from 1546 to the present. Works of art around the house include two portraits by Reynolds, others by Opie and Gand, and some local landscapes.

Open certain days, May–Sep.

HONITON
Town off A30, 16 miles (26km) NE of Exeter

Sometimes called the capital of East Devon, Honiton is famous for its lace and its memorable wide High Street lined with simple Georgian buildings. A prominent tower belongs to the odd neo-Norman 1830s church. Honiton lace was famous from Elizabethan times, and can be

seen in the museum. Tollgates and the tollhouse survive on the Axminster road.

Allhallows Museum
High St (next to parish church of St Paul)
Tel: 01404 44966

The museum has a wonderful display of Honiton lace, and there are lace demonstrations from June to August. The town's history is also illustrated, and the museum is interesting for its setting in a chapel built about 1200.

Open Etr–Oct, Mon–Sat.

Winter opening by special arrangement.

ILFRACOMBE
Town on A361, 9 miles (14km) N of Barnstaple

Until the 19th century this was a little fishing village with a sheltered harbour. The dramatic coastline with its rocky headlands and sheltered bays attracted visitors from the 1830s, and after the railways arrived in 1874 growth was fast. Now it is a mostly Victorian town, beautifully set out over the small hills and very unspoiled.

The fishing harbour (with boats to Lundy) is tucked behind a rocky headland which is crowned with a little medieval chapel (limited opening) that was used as a lighthouse from the 14th century. There are old houses and cottages along the harbour streets, but the High Street inland and most of the rest of the town is later Victorian, with plain, tall boarding-houses of brick. Many public gardens are laid out along the shore, some at amazing angles because of the little hills. The

Ilfracombe's sheltered harbour, with its tiny chapel

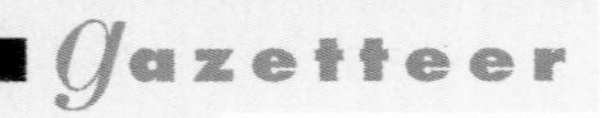

Tunnels have a Greek-style baths building of 1836 in front of the curious tunnels pierced through the rock to give access to little private beaches, linked by further tunnels.

Ilfracombe Museum is set in fine gardens, and has displays on Victorian residents and local history. Rolling Falls is a model of Clovelly, and Chambercombe Manor, just to the south, is a late medieval house, altered and restored.

One mile (2km) to the east is the pretty hamlet of Hele, with a big 18th-century working watermill.

Chambercombe Manor
1 MILE (1.5KM) E OF ILFRACOMBE, OFF A399
TEL: 01271 862624

This is one of England's oldest houses, *c*1066, although there are 16th and 17th-century additions. It boasts a priest's room, private chapel (dating from about 1066) and inevitably, a ghost. The garden includes an ancient wishing well and waterfowl ponds among its many charms. The bird sanctuary is home to many species of pheasant and peafowl.

Open Etr–Sep, certain times. Closed Sat.

Hele Mill
HELE BAY 1 MILE (1.5KM) E OF ILFRACOMBE, ON A399
TEL: 01271 863185 & 863162

Dating back to 1525, this mill still produces wheatflakes and different grades of wholemeal flour. Inside, many interesting items of mill machinery are on view. There are free pottery demonstrations before 11am, when visitors can also try their hands at throwing a pot of their own. Hand made pottery is on sale in the shop.

Open Apr–Oct, daily.

Ilfracombe Museum
RUNNEYMEDE GARDENS, WILDER RD
TEL: 01271 863541

Ilfracombe was an important trading port from the 14th to the 16th century and during the Napoleonic Wars became a popular resort. The history, archaeology, geology, natural history and maritime history of the area are illustrated here, along with Victoriana, costumes, photographs and china. There is also a brass-rubbing centre.

Open all year, at certain times.

Watermouth Castle
3 MILES (5KM) NE OF ILFRACOMBE, OFF A399
TEL: 01271 863879

Overlooking a beautiful bay, this 19th-century castle is one of North Devon's finest. It caters enthusiastically for the public, offering unique experiences in the main castle building as well as the lower courtyard and even the dungeons. There are continuous demonstrations of Mechanical Music, a model railway and the Watermouth Water Fountains. A special attraction is Gnomeland which offers a mine with a gnome's workshop, a chance to go panning for gold, and even radio controlled ducks. Project packs are available for educational visits.

Open Etr–Oct Sun–Fri. Limited opening off-season, please telephone for details.

LYDFORD
VILLAGE OFF A386, 8 MILES (13KM) N OF TAVISTOCK

From the 9th century Lydford was a fortified town, but now it is only a small village. The square castle (English Heritage) is early medieval, used as a prison. Lydford Gorge (National Trust) is a deep gorge cut by the river, rocky and woody, with narrow parts where the rock walls almost touch, waterfalls and deep pools. This is the best scenery in Devon. Lydford was the largest parish in England, covering most of Dartmoor.

Lydford Castle

The great square stone keep dates from 1195. It is not built on a mound, as it seems to be, but on earth which has been piled up against the walls. The upper floor was a Stannary Court, which administered local tin mines, and the lower floor was used to imprison those who broke the forest and stannary laws.

Open at all reasonable times.

Lydford Gorge
TEL: 01822 820441 & 820320

The spectacular gorge has been formed by the River Lyd, which has cut into the rock and caused swirling boulders to scoop out potholes in the stream bed. This has created some dramatic features, notably Devil's Cauldron close to Lydford Bridge. At the end of the gorge is the 90-ft (27-m) high White Lady Waterfall.

Open Apr–Oct, daily. Nov–Mar, waterfall entrance only.

A walk leads to the dramatic White Lady Waterfall

A woodland and riverside walk to the lovely beach at Heddon's Mouth, with wildlife interest well maintained between the contrasting environments of oak woodland and seashore.

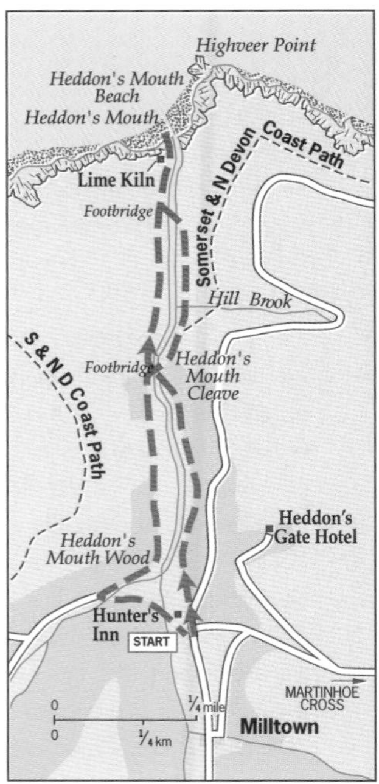

Grid ref: SS665482

INFORMATION

The walk is 2 miles (3km) long.
A straightforward and generally level walk along wide paths with some short inclines.
Very short road section; care needed on corners.
Good picnic area on river bank.
Pub and café at Hunter's Inn.
Toilets at Hunter's Inn Shop.
Dogs must be kept on leads.

START

All the roads to Hunter's Inn are single track with passing places; and include a 1 in 4 (25%) hill; great care needs to be taken.
From Combe Martin, turn off to the north along a side road just before leaving the village; from Lynton turn north off the A39 at Martinhoe Cross.

DIRECTIONS

Follow the track to the right of the Hunter's Inn. Go through a gate and follow the path bearing left at a fork. At the next fork, just past a wooden seat, either path can be taken: the left branch leads above the river while the path to the right climbs slightly on its way through the woods before the two link up again at a footbridge. Cross the footbridge and turn right to follow

A rustic bridge in the valley of the River Heddon

WHAT TO LOOK OUT FOR

You cannot miss the handsome peacocks at Hunter's Inn and the woods are full of less exotic but still fascinating bird life. Fast-moving dippers, with their distinctive white breasts, frequent the River Heddon. Butterflies, such as pearl-bordered fritillaries, inhabit the woodlands, and look out along the coast for the stiff-winged fulmar, a rather gull-like seabird.

the river downstream before passing through a gate; at the junction with the other path turn right. The path again follows the river downstream to reach a grassy open space just before another footbridge. Continue along the left bank above the river to the old lime kiln. The beach is easily reached from here, but be aware of the tide and don't wander far. Return to the nearest bridge. Cross over and follow the path upstream over a stony section, to reach the higher bridge. Cross this second bridge, then pass through the gate. Turn left at the junction and follow the path. On reaching the road turn left and walk back towards Hunter's Inn.

Heddon's Mouth

There are few beaches along the wild Devon coast and places like Heddon's Mouth have provided access to and from the sea for hundreds of years. The main trade was in coal and limestone, brought by ship from Wales for the kiln. Heddon's Mouth was also used by smugglers. The name Heddon comes from 'etin', the ancient name for giant.

Heddon's Mouth is in the joint ownership of the National Trust, Devon County Council and the Exmoor Society. The Exmoor Society was formed in 1958 after a successful campaign by lovers of the moor to prevent an area of the high moor called The Chains from becoming a conifer plantation.

Lime Kilns

The well-preserved lime kiln above Heddon's Mouth beach is typical of many round the Devon coast, often sited at coves and beaches where coal could be easily landed. Limestone was also brought in if there was no convenient local supply. The coal and limestone were burnt in layers utilising a simple draught system and the resulting lime was used by farmers to sweeten acidic soil.

Visitors view the old lime kiln at Heddon's Mouth

MORWELLHAM
Village off B3257, 4 miles (6km) SW of Tavistock

This village on the Tamar, was once a large port for copper, in the mid-19th century. Many historic features have been preserved and reconstructed, with rides into the copper mine, quays and ships.

Morwellham Quay
4 miles (6.5km) W of Tavistock, off A390
Tel: 01822 833808 & 832766 (Party bookings)

When copper was discovered in the hills near Tavistock the town reached new heights of prosperity. Morwellham was the nearest point to which sea-going ships could navigate, and became the greatest copper port in Queen Victoria's empire. Once the mines were exhausted the port area disintegrated into unsightly wasteland, until 1970 when a charitable trust was set up for its restoration. It is now a thriving and delightful open-air museum. Cottages have been faithfully renovated, and visitors can meet a blacksmith, cooper, assayer, quay workers and coachmen, all dressed in period costume to help recreate history in this picturesque old port. There are also underground rides into a copper mine, heavy horse-drawn wagons, slide shows and other displays. (Reduced operation during the winter months). Unspoilt countryside, riverside and woodland trails surround the museum.

Open all year. Closed Christmas week.

NEWTON ABBOT
Town off A380, 6 miles (9.5km) NW of Torquay

This little settlement at the head of the Teign estuary grew enormously after it became a railway centre in 1856. Medieval buildings can be found in the centre, but there are rows and rows of Victorian railway workers' housing. The 15th-century Bradley Manor is owned by the National Trust; Victorian Tucker's Maltings is still working.

OKEHAMPTON
Town off A30, 23 miles (37km) W of Exeter

Okehampton is a small market town with a large castle on the edge of Dartmoor. A little medieval church is prominent in the centre. The handsome granite town hall dates from 1685; most of the rest is Victorian or Edwardian. The shopping arcade (1900) is surprising in such a small town. The large medieval castle ½ mile (1km) south-west (English Heritage) has a really romantic setting in a wooded valley, and the Museum of Dartmoor Life is well worth a visit.

Okehampton Castle
Tel: 01837 52844

Set among richly wooded hills in the rolling Devon countryside, the size and strength of Okehampton Castle comes as something of a surprise. Okehampton's history has been relatively uneventful, and the only episode of national significance that occurred here was when one of its owners, Henry, Marquis of Exeter, was executed by Henry VIII for conspiracy in 1539, after which the castle was seized by the Crown and dismantled.

Okehampton Castle is, in fact, one of the largest and most extensive castle ruins in the West Country, and is sadly neglected by tourists. It

Okehampton Castle stands on the northern fringe of Dartmoor National Park

started as a simple mound, probably before 1070, and a stone keep was erected in the late 11th century. In the early 14th century a second building was added to the keep, with thick walls and fine round-arched windows. At the same time, other buildings were raised below the keep, producing an elongated enclosure protected by walls and steep slopes. These other buildings included kitchens, more accommodation, a solar and hall, guardrooms and a chapel. A gatehouse was also raised, connected to the rest of the castle by a long, narrow tunnel. Many of the buildings are in an excellent state of preservation, and this neglected castle is well worth a visit.

Open daily, Apr–Oct.

Museum of Dartmoor Life
The Dartmoor Centre, West St
Tel: 01837 52295

An attractive three-storey watermill houses this museum, and the Dartmoor Tourist Information Centre and working craft studios are to be found in an adjoining courtyard. There is a display of Victorian life, and descriptive reconstructions of local tin and copper mines are complemented by a geological display of the moor. Local history, prehistory, domestic life, industry and environmental issues are explored, and a 1922 Bullnose Morris farm pickup with a wooden back shares pride of place with an ancient David Brown tractor in the agricultural section. Features include a reconstructed blacksmith's forge and wheelwright's shop, a cider press and railway relics. Various craft events and demonstrations are held throughout the year.A shop sells crafts and books and an exhibition gallery holds regular displays.

Open Etr–Oct, Mon–Sat; also Sun, Jun–Sep. Nov–Mar weekdays only. Closed 25 Dec–1 Jan.

A good, mostly level walk round the southern headland of the mouth of the river Yealm, passing through the charming creekside village of Noss Mayo. Most of the walk is along the broad and amenable Revelstoke Drive.

Grid ref: SX541466

INFORMATION

The walk is about 4 miles (6.5km) long.
Level, easy walking with a long upward incline at the finish.
Short section of quiet road walking.
Several stiles.
Pubs in Noss Mayo.
Good picnic spots along the first part of Revelstoke Drive and at Cellar Beach.

WHAT TO LOOK OUT FOR

Watch for boats and ships out to sea, and for yachts coming in and out of the River Yealm. Seabirds such as gulls, terns and gannets also pass along the coastal section. This area was a managed rabbit warren in the 19th century and rabbits can still sometimes be seen on the grassy open spaces. The woods on the second section of the walk are full of birds and plant life.

The delightful creekside village of Noss Mayo

START

The National Trust car park is reached from Noss Mayo (see page 36) via Netton Farm. The way is signposted from Noss Mayo but the provision of signs is not particularly generous; Devon lanes can be confusing, particularly on the way back. Navigators should be on their toes!

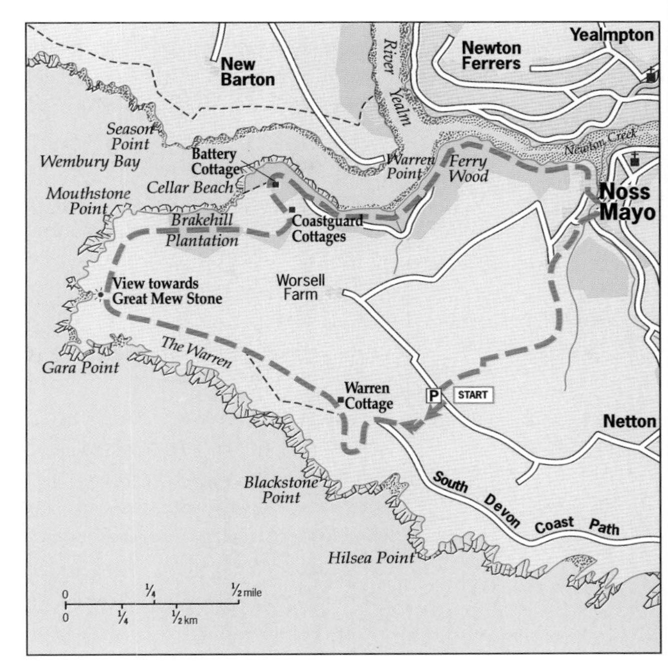

DIRECTIONS

Leave the car park through the gate in the far left-hand corner. Go down the lane and cross a stile to turn right onto the coast (superb views). At the entrance to the prominent Warren Cottage, go left through a gate and along a short section of path, then through another gate to rejoin the broad drive. Follow the coast path over a few stiles, continuing round Gara Point and enter Brakehill Plantation. Go through a gate by a National Trust sign indicating the end of The Warren property and continue past some old coastguard houses. Just past here a path leads down quite steeply to the left to Cellar Beach, which is worth visiting.

Continue on the main path past the distinctive Battery Cottage. The way leads on, with lovely views of the river, through Passage Wood and Ferry Wood to reach the surfaced lane. Follow this for about ½ mile (1km) into Noss Mayo.

Continue to the head of Noss Creek. Bear left up the road, then go right to reach a large car park with an adjoining children's play area. Beyond the car park entrance follow the rough track uphill, past hillside cottages on the right, and continue for about ½ mile (1km), passing a farmhouse on the right. At a T-junction turn left to reach the car park almost immediately on your right.

The Revelstoke Drive

Revelstoke Drive is a remarkable Victorian feature – the inspiration of Edward Charles Baring, Lord Revelstoke, who owned the surrounding Membland Estate. The Drive is part of a 9-mile (14.5km) circular carriageway round the estate, built near the end of the last century by local fishermen during the slack winters. Lord Revelstoke would drive his house guests by carriage round the drive to view his domain.

The Great Mew Stone

This rocky island lying to the east of Gara Point takes its name from the 'mewing' of the seabirds that have colonised it for centuries. The Mew Stone was occupied from 1774 when a convicted criminal was banished there with his family for a seven-year term. When the family eventually left, one daughter remained, married and raised a family there. The last known inhabitant kept a rabbit warren on the island during the early 19th century. Not surprisingly, he was also a smuggler!

NOSS MAYO
Village off B3186, 3 miles (5km) SW of Yealmpton

This small, rather remote fishing village on the Yealm estuary dates from medieval times and boasts several 1880s estate cottages and an elaborate church of the same date. The village's sheltered position and good anchorage on the River Yealm probably encouraged smuggling, which was rife along the South Devon coast in the 17th and 18th centuries.

(See alsoWalk: Noss Mayo and the Revelstoke Drive walk, p 34.)

OTTERTON
Village off B3178, 2 miles (3km) NE of Budleigh Salterton

Cob and thatch cottages can be seen down the wide main street, where there is also a stream. The village is also notable because of the working mill (see below).

Otterton Mill Centre
Off A376
Tel: 01395 568521

Mentioned in the Domesday Book, this water-powered mill grinds wholemeal flour used in the baking of bread and cakes sold on the premises. A gallery houses a series of exhibitions through the summer and autumn, and there are studio workshops for stained glass, pottery, woodturning and printing. There are long and short riverside walks, and an annual exhibition of furniture design from West Country workshops in October.

Open all year, daily.

OTTERY ST MARY
Town on B3174, 11 miles (17.5km) E of Exeter

This pretty little town, with its narrow twisting streets, boasts one of the finest churches in the country, dating from the mid-14th century. The plan of the large church is very elaborate, with a Lady Chapel. Flaming tar-barrel rolling is still practised annually on 5 November.

Cadhay
Near jct of A30 & B3167, 1 mile (1.5km) NW of Ottery over Cadhay Bridge
Tel: 01404 812432

This fine Tudor and Georgian house was begun in 1550 and stands around a delightful courtyard, walled in chequered flint and stone.

Open Jul–Aug Tue, Wed & Thu. Also Sun & Mon of late spring & late summer BHs, afternoons only.

Escot Aquatic Centre & Gardens
Fairmile
Off the A30 Exeter to Honiton road at Fairmile, signposted
Tel: 01404 822188

Escot House was built in 1837 after the original house was destroyed in a fire. The 54 acres (22ha) of landscaped parkland were designed and built, possibly by Capability Brown, before the Kennaway family, the present owners, moved into the estate 200 years ago. As well as the Victorian rose garden and extensive shrubbery with many fine specimen trees, you will also find a pair of otters, a troupe of wild boar, pets' corner and Vietnamese pot-bellied pigs. The aquatic centre is set in magnificent listed farm buildings, and houses an extensive range of spectacular tropical fish.

Open all year, daily.

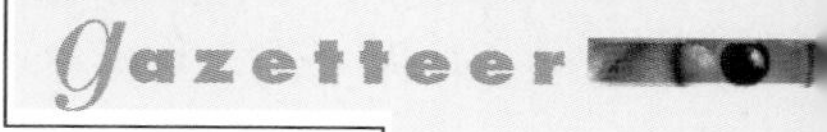

PAIGNTON
TOWN OFF B3022, 3 MILES (5KM) SW OF TORQUAY

Paignton was just a large village until the middle of the 19th century; from that time it began to be developed as a huge seaside resort because of its sandy beaches. Kirkham House (English Heritage), a late medieval stone house, and Oldway (now council offices), are the best buildings. Oldway is an imitation of Versailles, built in the late 19th century. Other attractions include Paignton Zoo, Torbay Aircraft Museum and Paignton and Dartmouth Railway.

Paignton & Dartmouth Railway
QUEENS PARK STATION, TORBAY RD
TEL: 01803 555872

Steam trains run for 7 miles (11km) from Paignton to Kingswear on the former Great Western line, stopping at Goodrington Sands, a popular beach, and at Churston, where there are connections with the ferry crossing to Dartmouth.

Special events are organised which appeal to families.

Open Jun–Sep daily & selected days Oct–Nov & Mar–May.

Paignton Zoo
TOTNES RD
TEL: 01803 527936

The zoo at Paignton offers an opportunity to see conservation in action. One of England's biggest zoos, it is sited in beautiful wooded 75-acre (30-ha) gardens. The zoo is home to over 60 endangered species, and is committed to working with good zoos around the world to secure their survival. New attractions include a huge area for African lions and Sumatran tigers, a fascinating walk-through aviary and a wetland wildlife exhibit. Other favourites include the 'Jungle Express' miniature railway, the 'Jolly Jungle' children's play area, and face painting.

Open all year, daily. Closed 25 Dec.

A steam train passes the beach at Goodrington Sands

In the space of a few easy miles, this scenic adventure transports you from the coastal estuary of a naval city, across viaducts of the old Great Western Railway, spanning beautiful wooded valleys, to the edge of rugged Dartmoor. Granite trails and sleepy Devon villages bring the rider to idyllic picnic spots on the banks of Burrator reservoir.

INFORMATION

Total distance
28¾ miles (46km), with 13 miles (21km) off-road.

Difficulty
Challenging

OS Maps
Landranger 1:50,000 sheets 201 (Plymouth & Launceston) and 202 (Torbay & South Dartmoor)

Tourist Information
Plymouth, tel: 01752 266030

Cycle Shops/Hire
Saddles & Paddles, Exeter, tel: 01392 424241; Breakthrough Mountain Sports, Plymouth, tel: 01752 795419

Nearest Railway Station
Plymouth (2 miles/3km)

Refreshments
Families are welcome in the Burrator Inn, Dousland, and the Skylark pub in Clearbrook has a special children's room, but the Royal Oak in Meavy does not allow children under 14. The Plym Valley Railway Cafe is open on Sundays only, but there are plenty of picnic spots along the route, especially at Burrator reservoir.

Saltram House, the setting for the film Sense and Sensibility

START

Follow signs to the Plym Valley Railway Co off the main A38 through Plymouth. Ample parking at the B&Q complex makes this the best starting point for the Plym Valley Cycle Way. Saltram House (NT) and grounds make an interesting 2-mile (3-km) southern extension, following the edge of the scenic Plym Estuary.

DIRECTIONS

1. From B&Q follow signs to the start of the trail between the Royal Marines base and the Plym Valley Railway Headquarters. After 1¼ miles (2km) of wooded cycling you reach Plym Bridge, site of the old station. About 300 yards (275m) further on, just before Plym Viaduct, access to Cann Wood offers 6 miles (9.5km) of off-road bike trails. Cann Quarry historic buildings are accessible below the first of three viaducts, all offering exceptional views. At Bickleigh a short signposted on-road section quickly rejoins the railway path which leads to a fourth viaduct offering distant views of Dartmoor.

After the over-head aquaduct, enter Brunel's Shaugh Tunnel (the walls are painted white but a torch is recommended). The trail ends after a further mile (1.5 km) with a switchbacked footpath, waymarked with red arrows, bringing you to Clearbrook, just a few metres from the Skylark pub. The Star Inn is down to the left.

2. Turn right, downhill, through pretty Hoo Meavy, forking right towards Cadover Bridge. At the top of the not unpleasant 875-yard (800-m) climb, glance back at the view before heading north towards Meavy. Pass the farmhouse B&B on the left, turn right after ½ mile (1km) towards Lovaton and look left across farming country to the unmistakeable jagged outline of

Meavy village green, near Yelverton

Pew Tor against the sky-line. At the T-junction just beyond Lovaton, turn right uphill then immediately left following the Sheepstor sign; Burrator dam can be seen across the valley. After ½ mile (1km), just past the clump of trees and Ringmoor Cottage, go right off the higher road (after the fork), following a bridlepath to a signposted gate in the fence. Note: this slightly strenuous 5-mile (8-km) off-road section can be omitted by a ½-mile (1-km) detour which leads straight to Nattor. Follow the wooden waymark posts for 1½ miles (2.5km) across open Ringmoor Down, wildest Dartmoor, to a second horse gate. Once through, head down towards Ditsworthy Warren House below. After exploring, fork left behind the enclosure to an obvious track (down to the right is the fledgling River Plym).

Continue up an ill-defined track to the left edge of the shadow valley passing the very tall standing stones which are off to the right. Over the rise, after about 1 mile (1.5km), take the broad sandy trail sharply back to the left, returning via a rocky descent of about 1¼ miles (2km), past the scout hut and ford. Rejoin the tarmac and turn right to Sheepstor, proceed for ½ mile (1km) following the stream.

3. Just beyond Sheepstor church, turn right on the perimeter road around Burrator reservoir. At the dam check the water level; bear straight on to the cattle grid ½ mile (1km) away, turning left, signed 'Meavy ¾', or make a diversion right for ½ mile (1km) to the Burrator Inn. In Meavy keep straight on towards Cadover (turn right for the Royal Oak pub). Avoid the deep ford by using the bridge. A 1:6 hill returns you to Lynch Common junction – follow signs for 1¼ miles (2km) over two junctions to Cadover Bridge. Cross the bridge, turn immediately left up the 'no through road', climbing for 875 yards (800m) with Trowlesworthy Tors on your left and the quarry on the right.

4. At Blackaton Cross, turn right through the small car park and on to the bridleway that leads off between the two vast china clay quarries. Stay off the quarry roads. High pressure water extraction work may be visible below. After 300 yards (280m) cross a quarry road and head diagonally right up towards the Saddlesborough Hill triangulation point, which is just visible over the crest, where you will be rewarded with an amazing panorama from Plymouth Sound to Cornwall. Also look for Brent Tor with its famous church on the top. Follow the descending path which leads directly towards Plymouth Sound, dropping to the right of Hawks Tor rocks to reach the road in ½ mile (1km). Cross the road, with more open ground for a short distance before emerging on tarmac at a cattle grid. Cross it, then turn immediately right, continuing to the T-junction at the very end. The road drops right down the hill (beware of the bends and narrow bridge as the road snakes speedily past Bickleigh Cottage at the bottom).

WHAT TO LOOK OUT FOR

Flora and fauna along the Plym Valley include wading shore birds in the lower reaches and tree pipits, jays and woodpeckers in the oak, ash and Douglas fir. Pink willowherb, primrose and wild garlic are also in the woodlands. Fallow deer are present but rarely seen by visitors in the valley. Heron occupy the skies over the reservoir and wheeling buzzard are also common over the moor. Riding to Saltram, reflect as you pass under the A38 on the awesome project that slid the flyover into position in one massive length. At Sheepstor search the churchyard for the granite tombstones of the white Rajahs of Sarawak; Sheepstor's connections with this distant far-eastern land are described inside the fascinating church.

5. Turn left and dismount for the steep ascent, which is known to the Commandos as 'Heartbreak Hill'. Near the top rejoin the Plym Valley Cycle Way, returning 3 miles (5km) to the start of the route.

Dartmoor

High, bleak and wild, Dartmoor is the only true wilderness in southern England. It is only too easy to get lost walking in these rolling granite uplands, especially when the weather is bad. Its association with endurance tests, and a tough prison, suits the moor well. Blanket bogs of peat cover most of the higher parts, with bare tors of granite at the very tops. These stark outcrops of the underlying rock are picturesque, if often windswept. The valleys too contain bogs.

As the many archeological remains indicate, Dartmoor was well populated until the end of the Bronze Age, when the climate deteriorated and the area became deserted moorland. Stone rows, cairns and hut circles all survive because they were built of the granite. The densest concentration is found in the southern valleys.

From medieval times Dartmoor has been worked for tin, usually by sorting the gravels in rivers. Streams were diverted for this, and there are ruins of many small buildings used on the moor.

Dartmoor became a National Park in 1951.

The pretty village of Sheepstor with Burrator reservoir in the background

PLYMOUTH
CITY OFF A38, SW OF EXETER

This is the largest city in south-west England, standing on a superb site flanked by the estuaries of the rivers Tamar and Plym. Plympton was the earlier settlement, but from the 14th century Plymouth took over.

The Hoe is the famous park and promenade overlooking Plymouth Sound, with wonderful views of the sea and wooded headlands. Drake's Island is in the middle, with the 1-mile (1.5-km) long breakwater (completed 1847) beyond. Stonehouse and Devonport are to the west. There are many memorials on the Hoe, including Smeaton's Tower (the Eddystone Lighthouse of 1759) and a statue of Sir Francis Drake, who famously completed his game of bowls before going off to defeat the Spanish Armada. Attractions include the Plymouth Dome with its high-tech displays, the Plymouth Gin distillery which is open to visitors, and the Plymouth Aquarium. Plymouth once had miles of elegant Regency terraces: some survive at the western end of the Hoe.

The huge citadel, with vast walls and an ornate gateway, is a barracks, built in 1666 and still in use. The Barbican is the old harbour area and has a rich history ranging from Elizabethan seamen to Francis Chichester's triumphant return. The *Mayflower* left for America from here in 1620, and there is an old fish market on the quay. The streets, some cobbled, are lined with old houses including the Elizabethan House, which is open. The 16th-century Merchant's House Museum can be found further into the town, as can the City Museum and Art Gallery.

The Barbican area is the old heart of Plymouth

Plymouth's centre was destroyed by bombing in World War II, and was replaced by a new grid. The ruins of Charles Church (1640s) remain as a memorial to the bombing. Some Victorian churches survived, and the 1870 guildhall was restored, but most of the centre is recent, with large, widely-spaced buildings. Plymouth today is the regional shopping centre, still closely involved with the Royal Navy as it has been since the 18th century, but it is also a thriving commercial centre and resort.

City Museum & Art Gallery
DRAKE CIRCUS
TEL: 01752 264878

The City Museum and Art Gallery is home to the Fine and Decorative Art Collection which includes paintings, prints and Reynolds family portraits, silver and Plymouth china, and the Cottonian Collection of Drawings, Sculpture and Books. There is a lively programme of art exhibitions, as well as archaeology, local and natural history displays, and the Discovery Centre with a 'hands-on' section for children. Lunchtime talks and concerts are also on offer, please telephone for details.

Open all year, Tue–Sat and BH Mon. Closed Good Fri & 25–26 Dec.

Merchant's House Museum
33 ST ANDREWS ST
TEL: 01752 264878

The largest and finest 16th-century house surviving in Plymouth. Restored and opened in 1976, the house tells the story of Plymouth through the old counting rhyme, 'Tinker, Tailor, Soldier, Sailor. . . '. More recently a Victorian schoolroom has been recreated and is available for group bookings.

Open Apr–Sep, Tue–Sat and BH Mon (summer).

Plymouth Dome
THE HOE
TEL: 01752 603300 & 600608 (RECORDED MESSAGE)

This high-tech visitor centre takes you on a journey through time, exploring the sounds and smells of an Elizabethan street, walking the gun-deck of a galleon, sailing with the epic voyages from Plymouth Sound, dodging the press gang, strolling with film stars on an ocean liner and witnessing the devastation of the Blitz. Use high-resolution cameras to zoom in on ships and shoreline, or access computers to identify naval vessels. You can examine satellite weather pictures as they arrive from space, keep up to date with shipping movements and monitor the busy harbour on radar. An excellent introduction to Plymouth and a colourful interpretation of the past.

Open all year, daily. Closed 25 Dec.

Smeatons Tower
THE HOE
TEL: 01752 603300

This famous lighthouse, a triumph of 18th-century engineering, was built on the treacherous Eddystone rocks 14 miles (22.5km) out at sea to the south-west of Plymouth. It was replaced by a larger lighthouse in 1882, and moved stone by stone to its present site on the Hoe.

Open Good Fri–Oct. Parties by appointment throughout the year.

The painted stairwell at Powderham Castle

POWDERHAM CASTLE
(SEE ALSO PAGE 14)
TEL: 01626 890243

One of the oldest living creatures in the world resides at Powderham Castle. Timothy, the Mediterranean spur-thighed tortoise, is 155 years old and happily inhabits the rose garden at the foot of the east tower. From here he can survey the gardens, parkland and the River Exe.

Powderham Castle, considerably older than it looks, has belonged to the Courtney family, Earls of Devon, for some 600 years. Most of the alterations and additions to the original house date from the 18th and 19th centuries, and it is the elegance of that era which Powderham reflects today.

Orginating in France, the Courtneys were related by marriage to the royal house of Valois, and the founder of this line came to Britain with Eleanor of Aquitaine. Later Courtneys have included an Archbishop of Canterbury, a founder Knight of the Garter, and even an Heir Presumptive to the throne of England. And yet, if you ask today about famous members of the family, they are just as likely to mention their beloved elderly tortoise as any of these illustrious ancestors! There are many family portraits around the house, including a rather crowded painting of the 2nd Viscount, his wife and their family of 13 daughters and one son. It was the son, the 3rd Viscount, who was instrumental in reviving the Earldom of Devon which had been in abeyance since 1556.

Their Devon home reflects both the passage of time and the changing fortunes of the family from its 14th-century origins through the destruction and rebuilding of the Civil War period to the age of Victorian grandeur. The dining hall, though the most recent addition, is where the family history can be explored through a series of coats of arms going back to about AD1000. The Marble Hall is particularly interesting – it forms the lower half of the medieval Great Hall and still contains the three original arches, though they were plastered at a later date. This room would once have been as high as the staircase hall, with its fine mahogany staircase adorned with carved heraldic beasts and lavish plaster work; it was completed in 1755 at the cost of £355.14s. 0d.

Upstairs, the solar, once the family room of the medieval castle, has a charming collection of toys including a model house which was made by a retired estate worker. The rest of the house is an enchanting mixture of original medieval features, family portraits, splendid 18th-century decoration and little curiosities such as the narwhal's horn in the first library (listed in old inventories as a unicorn's horn), and the peacock ornament from the Empress of China's sedan chair at the top of the grand staircase.

Open Apr–Oct; closed Sat.

SIDMOUTH

TOWN ON B3175, 13 MILES (21KM) E OF EXETER

This charming Regency seaside resort is set in a narrow valley between high red sandstone cliffs. From having been merely a little fishing village until the late 18th century, Sidmouth then developed quickly as a select resort. The town still has quantities of Regency buildings, most of them featuring stucco decoration. Elegant villas and quirky Gothic-windowed cottages – some large, some thatched – are still surrounded by green spaces. The little Esplanade has terraces too. The infant Princess Victoria was staying here with her parents when her father died. Her presence added to the fashionable appeal of the town, and she contributed towards the rebuilding of the church in 1860.

A pretty walk up the River Sid leads to Sidford, once a hamlet on the main road, now joined to Sidmouth. There is a medieval bridge over the river, and the Donkey Sanctuary is to the east.

There is a local museum, and an International Folk Festival is held every August.

Sidmouth Museum

CHURCH ST

TEL: 01395 516139

Located in an elegant Regency house next to the parish church, the museum contains an interesting collection of local prints, as well as many mementoes of Sidmouth's heyday as a Victorian resort, a costume section and an excellent display of old lace. Guided town strolls, lasting approximately two hours, depart from the museum on Tuesdays and Thursdays at 10.15. Lace-making, craft demonstrations, and special exhibitions are also held, please telephone for details.

Open Etr–Oct daily at certain times. Other times by appointment.

SLAPTON

VILLAGE OFF A379, 5 MILES (8KM) SW OF DARTMOUTH.

This pretty village lies just inland, and is dominated by the 80-ft (24-m) ruined tower from a chantry. Slapton Ley is a strange lake, separated from the sea by a shingle bank. The long sandy beach has an obelisk commemorating the use of the area by the American army in 1944 rehearsing for the D-Day landings; 3,000 people were evacuated for ten months for this purpose, and the monument was presented to the local people in recognition of their contribution.

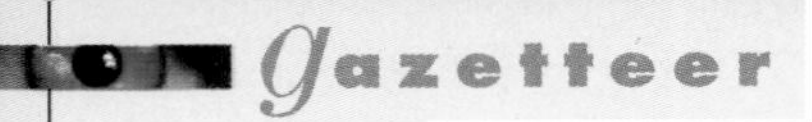

SLAPTON SANDS
5 MILES (8KM) SW OF DARTMOUTH.

The sea has piled up a long, straight bar of shingle that stretches north of Start Point. The A379 road from Kingsbridge to Dartmouth runs along the shore over Slapton Sands – which are actually shingle, though there is sand here at low tide. On the beach grow such plants as sea radish and sea dock, and a monument recalls that this part of the South Hams area of South Devon was taken over as a training ground for American troops preparing for the Normandy beaches.
Behind and sheltered by the shingle ridge is the freshwater lagoon of Slapton Ley, a mile or so long, up to 10ft (3m) deep and covering about 270 acres (110ha). A nature reserve, it is rich in fish and plant life. The northern end is thick with reeds and willow. Great crested grebe, stonechat, goldcrest, coot and mallard breed here, migrant birds rest here in spring and autumn, and in winter huge flocks of gulls gather on the beach and the Ley.

SOUTH MOLTON
TOWN ON B3227, 11 MILES (17.5KM) E OF BARNSTAPLE

This is a true market town, with a dense square in the centre packed with Georgian and Regency buildings. The Guildhall of 1740 arches over the pavement. There is a classical pannier market dating from 1863, and a local museum. The International Animal Rescue is at Ash Mill. Near by are Quince Honey Farm, Hancock's Devon Cider and Clapworthy Mill.

Quince Honey Farm
NORTH ROAD, 1½MILES (2.5KM) W OF A361
TEL: 01769 572401

This is the largest bee farm in Britain. Visitors can view the honey bees without disturbing them, in a specially designed building with glass booths and tunnels. Observation hives enable visitors to see into the centre of the colony and view larvae and newly-hatched bees in the cells of the comb. Even the queen may be seen at the very heart of the hive. The farm shop sells a wide range of honey, including the local heather honey, as well as pure beeswax candles and polish.

Open daily, Apr–Oct; shop only, Nov–Etr. Closed 25–26 Dec & 1 Jan.

Water lilies on the lake at Slapton Ley

South Molton Museum
Town Hall, The Square.
Tel: 01769 572951

The museum is in part of the town hall, a Portland stone-fronted building erected in about 1743. The entrance is through an open arcaded frontage. In the museum are objects relating to local history such as old charters, weights and measures, old fire engines and a giant cider press. There are monthly art and craft displays.

Open Mar–Nov, most days at certain times.

STARCROSS
Village on A379, 3 miles (5km) N of Dawlish

This riverside hamlet is situated on the Exe estuary, with passenger ferries in summer to Exmouth. The Brunel Pumping Station was one of ten on the short-lived (1846-7) 'atmospheric' railway built by Brunel from Exeter to Plymouth, worked by vacuum in the rails.

(See also Cycle ride: Exminster to Dawlish, page 14.)

START POINT
Headland off A379, SE of Hallsands.

This prominent headland marks the south-western corner of Devon, with a lighthouse dating from 1836. The South West Coast Path follows the wild and rocky coastline around the Point; the nearby village of Hallsands was destroyed by a storm in 1917, and is now almost deserted.To the north is the nature reserve of Slapton Sands.

(See also Slapton Sands, page 36).

The Tarka Trail is a 180-mile (290-km) long footpath which explores the area described by Henry Williamson in his 1927 nature tale, Tarka the Otter*; the lovely southern part of the trail, included here, runs along a former railway track. This ride goes from Barnstaple to Bideford, with the option to extend it as far as Old Torrington Station. It is flat, and provides safe, easy cycling for families.*

INFORMATION

Total Distance
18 miles (29km); with optional extension to 29 miles (46.5km).

Difficulty
Easy

OS Map
Landranger 1:50,000 sheet 180 (Barnstaple & Ilfracombe)

Tourist Information
Barnstaple, tel: 01271 388583

Cycle Shops/Hire
Tarka Trail Cycle Hire, Railway Station, Barnstaple, tel: 01271 24202; Bideford Bicycle Hire, Bideford, tel: 01237 424123

Nearest Railway Station
Barnstaple

Refreshments
Pubs and cafés in Barnstaple and Bideford; the Puffing Billy pub at old Torrington Station welcomes families.

The Tarka Trail by the river at Fremington Quay

Barnstaple bridge across the River Taw

START
Barnstaple is at the end of the Taw estuary, and lies on the A361 between Tiverton and Ilfracombe. Begin the ride from the Barnstaple railway station car parking area. This is on the south side of the River Taw, just off the B3233 after the river bridge.

DIRECTIONS
1. Leave the station car park and go under the B3233 viaduct, to pass through a gateway on to a track on your left – this is the Tarka Trail. Follow this track for 3 miles (5km) to Fremington Quay. Overlooking the River Taw, this is a pleasant place to pause and admire the many boats in the creek.

2. Continue through a cutting, and go straight on to Lower Yelland, where there is the site of an old power station. There is a nature reserve in the marshy bay. Continue and where the trail begins to bear left, look across the Taw to see Chivenor Airfield, which has a long history of civilian and military flying.

3. Follow the trail towards Instow, with good views of the open sea towards Lundy Island and Appledore on the opposite side of the River Torridge. Just before Instow, the track passes through a lit tunnel, to arrive at the level-crossing gates. There is still a signal box at this junction; it is looked after by local enthusiasts (who would dearly like to reinstate the railway line), and is sometimes open to view. (In summer you can catch the ferry from Instow Quay across to Appledore and back.)

4. Leave Instow and follow the track southwards beside the River Torridge. On the opposite bank is Northam. Pass under the A39 to reach a settlement with the quaint name of East-the-Water; beyond this, for contrast, is the old Bideford bridge, with its many arches.

5. Reach the site of the old Bideford station, where snacks and souvenirs are sold from an old railway carriage. Just across the bridge is the town of Bideford, and its many attractions could make it the end of your ride south. Retrace the outward journey to return to the start.

6. To extend the ride, you can continue on the Tarka Trail for

another 5 miles (8km) or so of attractive scenery and woodland; cross the Land Cross iron bridge, go through a tunnel, and cross three more bridges before reaching the Old Station at Great Torrington (now a cheerful pub).

WHAT TO LOOK OUT FOR

The Tarka Trail celebrates the story of an otter, but don't expect to see one – otters are very shy creatures, and while they do still live on the rivers and streams of Devon, you will be lucky to see more than footprints in the mud. However, there is plenty of other wildlife to look out for, especially wading birds, such as oystercatchers, curlew, dunlin, ringed plover and avocet who flock to the rich mudflats of the Taw estuary. Across the estuary, the sand dunes of Braunton Burrows are a nature reserve.

PLACES OF INTEREST

Barnstaple

The busy centre for north Devon, Barnstaple is one of the oldest boroughs in the country. A magnificent 16-arch bridge, dating from the 16th century, spans the River Taw here, just before it broadens into the estuary. The castle mound, opposite the Civic Centre, is an indication of the fortifications which once surrounded the town. Don't miss the vast, covered Pannier Market, and look out for the oddly twisted spire of St Peter's, the parish church, apparently struck by lightning in 1810.

Chivenor Airfield

In 1940 the small grass aerodrome here was developed into a modern airfield with permanent buildings, hangers and runways. With its proximity to the coast, it was used extensively by Coastal Command of the Royal Air Force in their work in the Western Approaches during World War II. An unexpected gift from the enemy came in the form of a Junkers Ju 88A 5 aircraft which landed at Chivenor, mistaking the base for one in France. As a result of recent cutbacks, the station is to close, and be left on a care and maintenance basis. Only the Air/Sea Rescue helicopters of 22 Squadron will remain.

Fishing boats at the quayside at Bideford

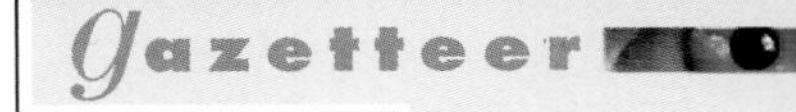

TIVERTON
TOWN ON A396, 12 MILES (19KM) N OF EXETER

In medieval times Tiverton's wealth was based on clothmaking; there are many later 18th-century buildings, and a fine early 18th-century church. Tiverton Castle has a medieval gateway, and there is a richly decorated porch of 1517 on the medieval church close by. West Exe, across the river, has much mid-19th-century housing, built for the textile workers. Tiverton museum has rural displays, and the Grand Western Canal basin, uphill from the town, is a mooring place for decorative barges; it is now a country park.

Tiverton Castle
TEL: 01884 255200

Dating from 1106, the castle dominates the river Exe. It was originally moated on three sides with the Exe as the fourth defence. One circular Norman tower remains of the original four, and there is also a medieval gatehouse with walls 5ft (1.5m) thick. The castle was a Royalist stronghold during the Civil War but was taken by the Parliamentarian Army in 1645. The tower houses a fascinating clock collection, and one of the finest collections of Civil War armour and arms in the country.

Open afternoons Apr–Jun & Sep, Sun, Thu & BH Mon's only; Jul & Aug, Sun–Thu.

Tiverton Museum
SAINT ANDREW
TEL: 01884 256295

This large and comprehensive museum consists of eight galleries and is housed in a restored 19th-century school. The numerous local exhibits include the Heathcote Lace Gallery featuring items from the local lacemaking industry (started by John Heathcote). There is also an agricultural section with a collection of farm wagons and implements. Other large exhibits include two waterwheels and a railway gallery that houses a GWR 0-4-2T Locomotive No. 1442, other railway items, and a display on the Grand Western Canal.

Open daily Mon–Sat. Closed 21 Dec–Jan.

The tower and lodge at Tiverton Castle

TORQUAY
TOWN ON A3022, 18 MILES (29KM) S OF EXETER

At the heart of the 'English Riviera', this huge seaside resort developed from the late 18th century. It has a very mild climate, encouraging exotic greenery and even palm trees, and a yachting and fishing harbour. The town centre is rather spoilt by big blocks of flats, but the outskirts still have dignified Victorian villas, set in large gardens with winding drives.

Many Victorian churches are scattered about the town, and an exotic pavilion of 1911 sits down by the harbour, with domes and tiles. There are parks and gardens everywhere, and the headland Torquay covers has small, dramatic hills, adding to the romantic effect. Rocky cliffs are all around, with sandy beaches.

Torre Abbey is unusual in being so close to the sea and has a 14th-century gatehouse, the rest of the buildings having been converted into a house in the 18th century. Torbay Museum displays local archaeology. In Kent's Caverns limestone caves, early prehistoric remains were found, along with the bones of extinct animals.

Babbacombe Model Village
HAMPTON AV, BABBACOMBE
TEL: 01803 328669

Set in 4 acres (1.5ha) of beautifully maintained, miniature landscaped garden, the village contains over 400 models and 1200ft (366m) of model railway. Authentic sound effects have been added. In summer, when the village is open until late, it is illuminated. 'City Lights', an evening illuminations feature, depicts Piccadilly Circus in miniature.

Open all year, daily. Closed 25 Dec.

Torre Abbey Historic House & Gallery
THE KINGS DRIVE
TEL: 01803 293593

Torbay's most historic building was founded in 1196 as a monastery and later adapted as a country house. It contains historic rooms, the Cary family chapel, mementoes of crime writer Agatha Christie, and mainly 19th-century paintings, sculpture, antiques, and Torquay terracotta pottery. The medieval monastic remains, which include the great barn, guest hall, gatehouse and undercrofts, are the most complete in Devon and Cornwall. Special exhibitions by local artists are held throughout the summer.

Open daily Apr–Oct.

TOTNES
TOWN ON A385, 7 MILES (11KM) W OF TORQUAY

Totnes is one of the best towns in the county, dense but on a human scale. The High Street runs down the hill, closely packed with buildings from the 16th century onwards. Some are picturesquely carried on pillars over the pavement, and the striking Eastgate (remodelled in 1837 and damaged by fire in 1990) stands over the road. The 16th-century buildings include the pillared Guildhall and timber-framed houses. Totnes Museum is located in a fine Elizabethan town house built by a rich merchant. The castle (English Heritage) at the top of the town still has an impressive motte with a 14th-century shell keep on

A ferry on the River Dart at Totnes

top, and the church has a handsome 15th-century 120-ft (36-m) tower and an outstanding stone screen of 1459. Totnes is at the lowest bridging point on the River Dart, with a handsome stone bridge of 1826 alongside the new one, built in 1982.

Other attractions in the town include the Devonshire Collection of Period Costume.

Guildhall
RAMPART WALK, OFF HIGH ST
TEL: 01803 862147

Originally the refectory, kitchens, brewery and bakery for the Benedictine Priory of Totnes (1088–1536), the building was established as the Guildhall in 1553 during the reign of Henry VIII. A magistrates court and a prison opened in 1624; during the same year the refurbishment of the council chamber, which is still used today, took place. There are also relics of the Civil War, and lists of the mayors since 1359.

Famous visitors to the Guildhall have included past monarchs such as Charles I and Charles II as well as the present monarch Queen Elizabeth II.

Open Apr–Sep, Mon–Fri at certain times.

Totnes Castle
TEL: 01803 864406

A classic example of the Norman motte-and-bailey castle, Totnes dates from the 11th century. The circular shell keep is protected by a curtain wall erected in the 13th century and reconstructed in the 14th. There are marvellous views from the walls of the keep across the town to the Dart valley.

Open Apr–Oct, daily; Nov–Mar, Wed–Sun. Closed 24–26 Dec & 1 Jan.

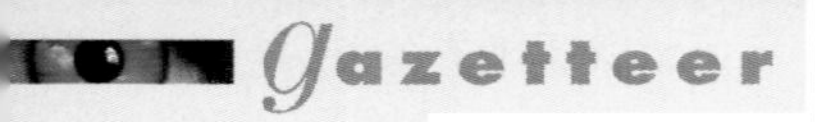

Totnes Elizabethan Museum
70 Fore St
Tel: 01803 863821

This four-storey, partly timbered house, complete with connecting gallery to an additional kitchen/buttery block, dates from about 1575. It has a cobbled courtyard and 16th-century fireplaces. It is now a museum of furniture, domestic objects, toys, dolls, costumes and archaeology. One room is dedicated to Charles Babbage who invented the ancestor of modern computers. There is a Tudor garden and Devon Record Office (study centre), and constantly changing displays of contemporary art and craft from the Totnes area.

Open Etr–Oct, Mon–Fri & BHs. Also Sat afternoons.

UFFCULME
Village off B3391, 5 miles (8km) NE of Cullompton

This large village, with a square at the centre, has a handsome church with an impressive early 15th-century fan-vaulted screen. Coldharbour Mill (1799) is now a working museum, producing woollen yarn.

Coldharbour Mill Working Wool Museum
Coldharbour Mill
Tel: 01884 840960

Originally an important centre for the wool trade, the Culm Valley now has only one working woollen mill. This was built as a grist mill in 1753, but was converted to a wool mill in 1797 by a Somerset woollen manufacturer, Thomas Fox. He added a large red-brick and stone factory in which serge, flannel and worsted yarn was produced for nearly 200 years. The mill closed in 1981 but was reopened as a Working Wool Museum. Visitors can watch every stage in the process of producing woollen cloth and yarn on the two working levels of the mill. There are also displays of interesting mechanical artefacts connected with the wool trade, plus a weaver's cottage, and dye and carpenters' workshops. Visitors can see the 18-ft (5.5-m) diameter water wheel awaiting restoration, and the 300-horsepower Pollit and Wigzell steam engine which powered the Mill until its closure. Knitting yarn and made-up garments can be bought in the mill shop.

Open Apr–Oct, daily. Nov–Mar, Mon–Fri at certain times.

YELVERTON
Small town on B3212, 5 miles (8km) SE of Tavistock

Yelverton lies on the edge of Dartmoor, but is rather suburban, being a dormitory town for Plymouth. The 1591 Plymouth Leat, made to carry water to Plymouth, runs to the south of the church, and the 1793 Devonport Leat to the north.

Paperweight Centre
4 Buckland Ter,
Leg O' Mutton (off A386)
Tel: 01822 854250

This unusual centre is the home of the Broughton Collection – a glittering display of paperweights of all sizes and designs. The centre also has an extensive range of modern glass paperweights for sale. Prices range from a few pounds to over £500. There is also a series of oil and watercolour paintings by talented local artists, a collection of which are scenes of Dartmoor.

Open all year, certain days.

CORNWALL

BODMIN
TOWN OFF A30, 18 MILES (29KM) E OF NEWQUAY

Bodmin was established in the 6th century when St Petroc settled here, and although it only feels like a market town it was the capital of Cornwall from 1835 until 1989.

St Petroc's Church reflects Bodmin's importance in medieval times, being the largest church in the county. It mostly dates from the late 15th century. There is a holy well near by.

Bodmin's streets are narrow and hilly. At the centre are the Victorian buildings for the courts. The market of 1839 includes bulls and rams in the decorative frieze. The big memorial obelisk of 1856 on the hill above the town is a prominent feature.

Bodmin Museum has displays on the area, and the prison of 1855 is also a museum. The Duke of Cornwall's Light Infantry Museum is located in the Victorian barracks. Bodmin and Wenford Railway runs steam trains to Bodmin Parkway, with stations for Cardinham Woods and Lanhydrock House (National Trust, 2½ miles/4km south-east). This is the grandest house in Cornwall, built in the 17th century and 1880s with lovely grounds. Pencarrow House (4 miles/6.5km north-west) is Georgian and handsome, with woodland gardens.

The stately formal gardens at Lanhydrock House

Bodmin Moor
REGION IN SW ENGLAND

About 100 square miles (258sq km) of moorland is cut across the middle by the A30. The highest and wildest parts are in the north – Rough (pronounced Row) Tor, and Brown Willy which is Cornwall's highest point at 1,377ft (418m). Many prehistoric remains are preserved on the moor, including standing stones, cairns, stone circles and hut circles.

Lanhydrock House
TEL: 01208 73320

Lanhydrock is approached along an avenue of beeches through a wooded park. It looks Tudor, but only the charming gatehouse, entrance porch and north wing date from the 16th century. The rest was rebuilt after a fire in 1881, and the house now gives a vivid picture of life in Victorian times. The 'below stairs' sections are particularly interesting and include a mighty kitchen, larders, dairy, bakehouse, cellars, and servants' quarters. Notable among the grander rooms is the long gallery, which has a moulded ceiling showing Old Testament scenes. The windows overlook the formal gardens with their clipped yews and bronze urns; the higher garden, famed for its magnolias and rhododendrons, climbs the hillside behind the house.

House open Apr–Oct daily; closed Mon, but open BH Mon. Gardens open daily. Winter Gardens Nov–Mar during daylight hours.

Bodmin and Wenford Railway
TEL: 01208 73666

The Bodmin and Wenford Railway offers a unique opportunity to compare the most modern of rail services with the nostalgia of the age of steam. It is the only preserved railway which is served by 125-mph (200-kph) High Speed Trains, and after being whisked from London Paddington or Edinburgh, passengers can cross a covered footbridge at Bodmin Parkway to an island platform from which Bodmin and Wenford trains depart. The 3½-mile (5.5-km) line, originally opened by the Great Western Railway in 1887, is the only standard gauge preserved railway in Cornwall, and recalls the days when the county was served by a fine network of picturesque branch lines to many of the principle resorts and market towns.

As the branch line turns away from the main line, it crosses a five-arch viaduct across the River Fowey, which rises on Bodmin Moor, then begins a taxing climb through wooded cuttings towards the one intermediate stop at Colesloggett Halt. This was built by the Bodmin and Wenford to serve a network of paths created by the Forestry Commission through nearby Cardinham Woods. The railway's guide book contains a description and a map of the woods showing the four routes through them; cycles can be hired at the entrance and refreshments are available at an adjacent café. The climb continues through banks of bracken and foxgloves with fine views northwards

A train passes Charlie's Gate on the Bodmin and Wenford Railway

over the fields to Bodmin Moor. On the outskirts of Bodmin the railway's largest steam locomotive, Southern Railway West Country class No 34007 Wadebridge, may be glimpsed on the east side, undergoing restoration beside the Fitzgerald Lighting factory. A little farther on are the redundant barracks of the Duke of Cornwall's Light Infantry. In 1944 the railway brought Field Marshall Montgomery and General Eisenhower to visit the regiment.

As the train enters the station after the 25-minute slog uphill (it takes only 20 minutes going back), a line swings in from the left. This was the link to Boscarne Junction and Wadebridge, which the Bodmin and Wenford hopes to re-open in order to relieve roads of china clay lorries as well as to take passengers to the Camel Trail. The attractive terminus at Bodmin is a 25-minute walk from the start of this popular trail which extends for 15 miles (24km) to the sea at Padstow. Cycles can be hired in Wadebridge, which is linked by bus to Bodmin and Padstow.

The train operates daily Jun–Sep; also on certain days in winter.

BOSCASTLE

VILLAGE ON B3263, 5 MILES (8KM) N OF CAMELFORD

This is the most dramatic of all the Cornish harbours: a dog-leg through the black cliffs, with small jetties in the inner part. The wild coastal scenery contrasts with the popular walk up the sheltered wooded Valency Valley to St Juliot. The whole area is closely associated with Thomas Hardy, and features in his novels and poetry.

BUDE

TOWN OFF A39, 15 MILES (24KM) NW OF LAUNCESTON

The only port on the harsh northern Cornwall coast, Bude developed faster after the Bude Canal to Launceston was built in the 1820s. The impressive sea lock survives (as well as a couple of miles of the canal), but the town now relies on its stretches of sandy beaches for most of its trade. The arrival of the railway in the 1880s (now closed) put the canal out of business and brought the holiday-makers.

This walk includes the wide open spaces of Crantock beach and its undulating dunes, with striking cliff-top views of Piper's Pool. The village of Crantock, with its many fine features, is also visited.

START

West Pentire is reached by turning off the A3075 just over a mile (1.5km) south of Newquay. There is a large car park.

Grid ref: SW776606

INFORMATION

The walk is 3 miles (5km) long.
Level most of the way but with one or two short flights of steps.
No road walking other than in Crantock and West Pentire.
A few stiles to cross.
Picnic on the beach.
Pubs and refreshments at Crantock and West Pentire.
Seasonal toilets at Crantock beach; all year toilets at Crantock.

DIRECTIONS

Down the road from the car park entrance turn left at the junction, signposted 'Vugga Cove'. Go through a gate just past some houses and follow the broad track. Bear sharp right and go through the gate. At the fork, go right and down over a stile. After about 50 yards (46m), descend a short flight of stone steps. Continue along the coast path and at a slight incline turn left and cross below a putting green. After 100 yards (90m) cross a granite stile and turn left at a fork to reach Pusey's Steps. The main path crosses a plank bridge, then climbs the flight of steps (good views). Continue along the cliff-top

Piper's Pool and Crantock Bay

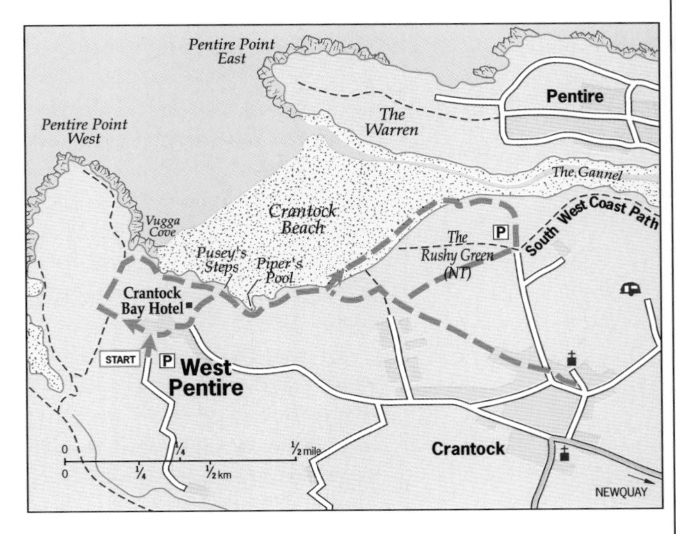

path and over a stile. At the far bottom corner of a field, the adventurous can drop 20ft (7m) down a sand dune onto the beach; otherwise continue round to the right to reach the beach by a gentler slope. At the far end of the beach, go up a wide break by a metal sign ('no river bathing') and down into the car park. Near the entrance on the right, by a National Trust marker, go up a path onto The Rushy Green. Follow a direct line across dunes aiming for a pink house with glass roof domes. To pass behind the house, follow a sandy path to a junction marked by two small fins of granite, then turn left through the zig-zag gate. At Boskenna House continue along the track (Green Lane). At the road junction, turn right into Crantock.

Retrace your steps to the pink house. Turn left at the junction by the zig-zag gate. Continue to a second junction and turn right, then immediately left. At the field edge, turn right and follow the path round the field back past Piper's Pool. Turn left at a junction after Pusey's Steps and follow a surfaced path to the road by the Crantock Bay Hotel. Cross, and turn right to reach the car park.

Pusey's Steps

This rocky access to the beach was reputedly used by a priest, Dr Pusey, who lived in the old Manor House at West Pentire, and who may well have been involved in the prolific smuggling which went on hereabouts. His ghost, said to be fairly active around dusk, is considered to be friendly!

Crantock's church, dedicated to St Carantoc dates from the 13th century

Crantock

This delightful old village was a major commercial centre and port long before Newquay developed. Schooners off-loaded just across the river, and barges would then transport the cargo for several miles up river. The Gannel is a lovely river but a dangerous one – warning notices against swimming should be heeded.

WHAT TO LOOK OUT FOR

The Rushy Green has a mass of flowering plants typically found in sand dunes, including marram grass, sea stock and sea sandwort. In the centre of Crantock are a holy well and the charming Round Garden; behind the church find the old village stocks and learn about the resourceful wickedness of an 18th-century smuggler!

CAERHAYS CASTLE
Gorran, 6 miles (9.5km) S of St Austell
Tel: 01872 501310

Caerhays is a name which was known at the time of the Domesday Book, and though the castle has all the appearance of a great Norman fortress, it is actually a product of the 19th century. It was built for one John Bettesworth Trevanion, who inherited Caerhays in 1801 at the age of 21. It is not clear why Trevanion felt the need for such an impressive new home on land which had been in the family since 1390, nor why he should choose John Nash – very fashionable and very expensive – as his architect. What is known for sure is that the cost of it ruined the family and by 1840 they retreated in debt to Paris, where John died.

The castle then stood empty, rapidly declining, for 13 years until it was bought by Michael Williams, a Cornish Member of Parliament, mine owner and industrialist. He and his son John are credited with the restoration of the castle, while the next two generations created and maintained the delightful gardens and grounds which surrounded it. Now in its fifth generation, the Williams family is still at Caerhays.

Today there are few reminders of the Trevanions, apart from a number of family portraits, and most of the furniture is modern.

Open between March and May, certain days.

CHYSAUSTER ANCIENT VILLAGE
Prehistoric site off B3311, 3 miles (5km) NW of Gulval
Tel: 01326 212044

This famous group of courtyard houses (English Heritage) was once believed to be Iron Age, but is now thought to be Roman. Eight drystone houses are arranged, mostly in pairs, along the oldest known village street in England. The walls survive to virtually their original height (nearly 6ft/2m in some places) and all that is missing are the roofs. One roof has been reconstructed.

Open Apr–Oct, daily.

(See also page 84.)

FALMOUTH
Town on A39, 12 miles (19km) S of Truro

Now the largest town in Cornwall, Falmouth is also one of the most recent. It was only a tiny village until the 17th century, and the deep-water natural harbour of Carrick Roads made it one of the largest trading ports in the country in the 18th century (see Pendennis Castle, below).The main street, with large Georgian and Victorian buildings, runs parallel to the shore and then further along turns its back on it. The early 19th-century Greek-style customs house has a brick chimney called the Queen's Pipe. The town church dates from 1660–1, with classical pillars and a plaster ceiling but medieval-style windows. Modern docks are tucked up under the headland, and the whole area is a popular yachting centre. Small passenger ferries run to St Mawes and to Flushing. The railway of 1863 made the town, with beaches on its southern side, into a resort. An art gallery and the Cornwall Maritime Museum are based here.

Cornwall Maritime Museum
TEL: 01326 316745

The museum is situated in the building which once housed the offices of the Packet Services. It gives a fascinating introduction to all aspects of Cornish maritime heritage, from sailors' superstitions through shipbuilding to smugglers. The history of the Falmouth packet ships is covered in detail in a special gallery, and there is a good collection of model ships of all types along with nautical artefacts in other galleries.

Open daily May–Sep; Oct–Apr, Mon–Sat.

Pendennis Castle
TEL: 01326 316594

This castle is a testament to the quality of the coastal defences erected by Henry VIII. The well-preserved granite gun fort and outer ramparts with great angled bastions defended the castle against invasion from the sea, but it was captured from the land after a long siege during the Civil War.

Open all year, daily. Closed 24–26 Dec & 1 Jan.

The inner keep and curtain wall of Pendennis Castle at Falmouth were built by Henry VIII to guard the entrance to the Carrick Roads.

FOWEY
TOWN ON A3082, 10 MILES (16KM) S OF LOSTWITHIEL

The steep, narrow streets of this pleasant old town plunge down the hillside above a lovely, yacht-crowded haven on the estuary of the River Fowey. Blessed with one of the best natural harbours on the south coast, Fowey (the name is pronounced to rhyme with 'toy') was an important port in the Middle Ages, on the trade route between mainland Europe and Ireland which crossed Cornwall overland to the Camel estuary. Its piratical seamen, the 'Fowey Gallants', were not averse to preying on ships in the English Channel and even raiding the French coast, sometimes provoking fierce retaliation – the French came and burned the town down in 1457. In the 19th century local ships traded to the Mediterranean and across the Atlantic, and Fowey became a china clay port. The parish church of St Fimbarrus has some fine monuments to the Rashleigh family, whose 15th-century town house is now the Ship Inn. The Lugger Inn is a 17th-century hostelry, the town hall in Trafalgar Square – now housing a museum – dates from the 1790s, and there are many other interesting old buildings.

FOWEY'S LITERARY CONNECTIONS

The wealthy merchant dynasty of Rashleigh had their country house outside Fowey at Menabilly. It was later for many years the home of Daphne du Maurier, who dearly loved this part of Cornwall and included references to it in many of her novels.

A delightful walk on St Mary's, the largest of the Scilly Isles, through quiet water meadows and on to a safe beach, then out to Peninnis Head with its fantastically shaped boulders. The walk can easily be included as part of a day-trip from the mainland.

Grid ref: SV903105

START

Hugh Town is the main settlement on St Mary's. Start the walk from the top end of High Street by the Bishop and Wolf pub.

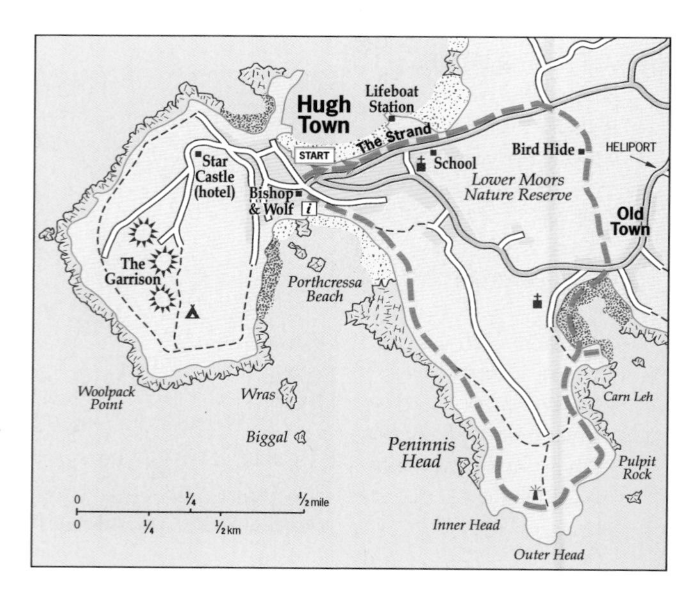

DIRECTIONS

Where the road forks in front of the pub, take the left fork and keep left at the next fork by the telephone boxes. Walk along The Strand, past the Customs House on the left, and continue uphill past the school and on down the left-hand pavement of Telegraph Road. At the end of the houses after 250 yards (230m), at a junction with a side road to the left, cross the road and go over a broken stone stile onto a signed path through the Lower Moors Nature Reserve. Where the path leaves the Reserve (after about ½ mile/1km) continue along a road between bungalows to Old Town. Cross the road to the beach.

From the far left (east) end of the beach go down the slipway steps and follow the sandy track along the beach to pass the church. Climb the rocks at the end of the beach onto the open cliff and follow the path. Explore the rocks of Carn Leh before continuing along the coast path, taking the lower left fork after about 500 yards (460m) to Peninnis Lighthouse. The surrounding rocks include the large protruding flat rock known as Pulpit Rock. Continue along the coast path from the lighthouse for about ½ mile (1km) to Porthcressa Beach. The start point is reached by walking down the road behind the information office and toilets on the beach front, and then along Silver Street to High Street.

INFORMATION

The walk is just over 3 miles (5km) long.The terrain is Level on the inland section and moderately undulating on the coastal section. Some road walking is involved, but there are pavements. Refreshments are available at the Café/restaurant at Old Town. Dogs are banned from Old Town beach and Porthcressa beach from May to September.

Birds galore

Small islands are often a paradise for birds, but the Scilly Isles are very special. They are particularly famous as staging posts for migrating birds during spring and autumn, when birdwatchers are sometimes able to spot rare species. At all times of the year there are opportunities for sightings of numerous seabirds including herring gulls, shags and oystercatchers with their distinctive black and white plumage and orange beaks. In Lower Moors there are snipe, moorhens and mallards.

A notable feature of Scillonian birdlife is the remarkable tameness of the songbirds resident in the islands,which include the song thrush and robin.

WHAT TO LOOK OUT FOR

There is a variety of birds to be seen in the Lower Moors reed beds, with a bird hide just off the path. The marine life of these islands is among the best in Britain, and at Old Town Beach there are a number of fascinating rock pools containing small fish like blennies as well as sea anemones, starfish, porcelain crabs and much more.

Porth Cressa and Hugh Town from Peninnis Head

Peninnis Rocks

The fantastically shaped granite rocks and headlands at Peninnis have been sculpted by the wind and water. Though the hollows in the rocks are caused by rain water, which has slowly worn out the basin shapes over many centuries, local legends suggest they may have been created by Druids for blood sacrifices! Individual rocks in the area have wonderful names like Kettle and Pans, and Tooth Rock, while caves and inlets include Big and Little Jolly, Sleep's Abode and Izzicumpacca. Watch out for seabirds, such as gannets, flying past the headland.

GWEEK
VILLAGE OFF B3293, 3 MILES (5KM) E OF HELSTON

This pretty village at the head of the woody Helford estuary was a port until the river silted.

National Seal Sanctuary, Marine Animal Rescue Centre
TEL: 01326 221361

Here at the largest seal sanctuary in Europe an average of 30 sick and injured seals are rescued and cared for each year, and then returned to the wild when fully recovered. With 10 pools, and a host of seals and sea lions, the highlights of a visit are the daily feeding times (six in summer and four in winter). Other attractions include the main exhibition with static and audio-visual displays, the hospital, safari bus rides, gift shop, café, seasonal barbecue, guided nature trail walks during the summer months, extensive picnic and play areas, an underwater viewing observatory, and children's quiz trail with scratch cards. Open all year, daily. Closed 25 Dec.

HELFORD
VILLAGE OFF B3293, 6 MILES (10KM) E OF HELSTON

An idyllic, tiny village on the Helford estuary. The pretty cottages were described in Daphne du Maurier's novel *Frenchman's Creek* (1942).

ISLES OF SCILLY
ISLAND GROUP LYING W OF LANDS END

The Scillies are a group of well over 100 islands, lying 28 miles (45km) west of Lands End. Warmed by the Gulf Stream, they have a mild climate with exotic and sub-tropical plants, and flower-farming as an industry. The population of about 20,000 nearly all live on St Mary's. There is very little traffic, as visitors are not permitted to bring cars or caravans over.

Samson, once inhabited, now has only the ruins of cottages with hedges marking the outlines of ancient fields. Tean was once used for grazing, and people lived here in the summer, burning seaweed for

Beautiful sea views from the site of Halangy prehistoric village, St Mary's, Scillies

kelp. The ruined hermitage on St Helen's is reputed to be the oldest Christian building on the islands, built between Roman times and the 8th century. Western Rocks are renowned as a graveyard for ships through the centuries, and Eastern Isles are home to seabirds and seals. There are remains of a late megalithic settlement on Nornour. Bishop Rock, Britain's tallest lighthouse, is on the south-west tip of the Scillies, on the inhabited island of St Agnes. The Old Man of Gugh, a standing stone 9 feet (3m) high, was erected by Gugh's Bronze Age inhabitants.

Hugh Town is the capital of the islands; other inhabited islands are St Martin's and Bryher, where Bronze Age cairns are found.

The sport of gig-racing can be watched in the summer, and the pilot gig, *Klondyke*, built in 1873, is exhibited in St Mary's Museum.

Tresco
ISLAND OF THE SCILLY GROUP

The second largest of the Scilly isles, Tresco is a private estate with no cars, only farm tractors. The island is wild and barren in the north, while its central section has green fields and cottages. Tresco Abbey Gardens are world-renowned sub-tropical gardens, also housing the Shipwreck Museum at Valhalla, which contains figure-heads and sternplates from wrecks around the islands. Cromwell's Castle was built in 1651, and King Charles's Castle 100 years before.

Tresco Abbey Gardens
TEL: 01720 422849

Few gardens are reached by a more exciting journey than the Abbey Gardens on Tresco. There is a choice of either taking the *Scillonian* from Penzance, and then a launch from St Mary's, or a helicopter – also from Penzance – that lands directly at the garden gates. The gardens represent a remarkable work of construction by their founder, Augustus Smith, in 1834, and they are maintained today by his descendant, the present owner, R A Dorrien Smith.

Tresco lies in the Atlantic 30 miles (48km) off the coast of Cornwall and is warmed by the Gulf Stream. Although the temperatures in winter rarely fall below 10°C, exceptional sub-zero temperatures in January 1987 caused terrible damage to some of the sub-tropical plants. Of course, the wind is an ever-present enemy, and with great forethought, Augustus Smith provided his three great terraces, the Long Walk and the Middle and Top Terraces, with shelter-belts of Monterey cypress, tall hedges of holm oak and high, retaining walls. These also provide an effective setting for the granite house that he built near the ruins of a Benedictine priory.

The 14-acre (5.5-ha) gardens are home to many exotic plants, including the South African proteus, the tender geranium from Madeira, *G. maderense*, tall date palms from the Canary Islands and

the striking Chilean *Myrtus luma* which has orange-coloured bark. There are also acacias, eucalyptus and the New Zealand *Metrosideros tomentosa* which is 80ft (24m) tall, has a great number of aerial roots and produces crimson flowers in summer.

Around St Nicholas's Priory honeysuckles, the blue-flowering *Convolvulus mauritanicus* and the pretty Mexican daisy spill out of cracks in the ancient walls and arches, and there is a magnificent rock garden excavated into a 40-ft (12-m) cliff below. The Middle Terrace has an area known as Mexico, and is covered with the turquoise flowers of *Puya alpestris* from Chile. Further along, a stone summerhouse is overgrown with Burmese honeysuckle.

Open daily, all year.

LANDS END

HEADLAND ON A30, 8 MILES (13KM) SW OF PENZANCE

The most westerly point of mainland England draws countless visitors to its dramatic cliff scenery. On a clear day the Isles of Scilly, 28 miles (45km) away, can be seen together with the Wolf Rock Lighthouse and the Seven Stones Reef, where the oil tanker the *Torrey Canyon* met its end in 1967. The 200-acre (81-ha) site is the setting for wild coastal walks and amazing natural rock formations; and innovative exhibitions have been set up to trace the geology, wildlife and maritime history of the area. On the southernmost tip of the peninsula are two small smugglers' coves linked by a tunnel which local miners carved through the headland. The *Last Labyrinth*, *Man Against the Sea* and *Spirit of*

The wild scenery of Lands End holds a timeless appeal

Cornwall exhibitions can be seen along with an audio-visual show. Visitors can take a ride on the land train to the Land of Greeb with its animals, craftsmen and model village.

Open all year. Closed 24–25 Dec.

LAUNCESTON
TOWN OFF A30, 20 MILES (32KM) NW OF PLYMOUTH

Pronounced 'Lawnston', this is the gateway to Cornwall and was its county town until 1835. The high mound of the medieval castle (English Heritage), surmounted by a shell keep, dominates the town. One castle gatehouse survives, and another from the town walls. Of the steep streets, Castle Street has the best buildings: big 18th-century houses, some of brick. The outer walls of the 15th-century church are covered in decorative carvings, an amazing feat as they were built in hard granite. There is a narrow-gauge steam railway in the valley.

Launceston Castle
TEL: 01566 772365

Henry III had a younger brother named Richard who was a skilful politician, a cunning diplomat and wiser by far than his brother the King. Richard used his considerable talents to make himself one of the richest barons in the country – amassing far more wealth than Henry ever possessed – and with his wealth came a different sort of power. He was elected King of the Romans, and even tried to secure for himself the position of Holy Roman Emperor. In 1227, Richard was made Earl of Cornwall, and it was he who built the fine castle at Launceston.

Launceston is a good example of what is known as a shell keep, which consists of a circular wall with buildings inside. Inside this outer wall Richard built another tower, roofed over the space between the two walls, and added a fighting platform around the outside of the outer wall. After Richard's death in 1272, Launceston declined in importance as a military fortress, and by 1353 it was reported that pigs were endangering its foundations by trampling the moat. Launceston was also used as a prison; it is believed that George Fox, the founder of the Quakers, was held here for eight months in 1656.

Open Apr–Oct daily.

Launceston Steam Railway
TEL: 01566 775665

The Launceston Steam Railway links the historic town of Launceston with the hamlet of New Mills. Travelling through the glorious countryside of the Kensey Valley, the trains are hauled by locomotives built in Victoria's reign. Tickets are valid for unlimited travel on the day of issue, so you can break your journey at various points along the track. At New Mills there are a range of waymarked footpaths, a riverside picnic area and a water mill. Launceston Station houses railway workshops, a transport museum, gift shop and book shop.

Open certain days, Etr–Oct.

Passing no fewer than 35 farmyards, this pastoral journey explores little-known agricultural thoroughfares in the lee of the one-time Cornish capital, Launceston. En route you discover mischievous otters, the secrets of glass-blowing, a working steam railway, space-age windmills and at least one picture-postcard village. With Bodmin and Dartmoor constantly in view, the off-road stretch affords opportunities for likely wildlife sightings in the still forest.

INFORMATION

Total distance
29½ miles (47km), with 1 mile (1.5km) off-road

Difficulty
Moderate

OS Maps
Landranger 1:50,000 sheets 190 (Bude) and 201 (Plymouth & Launceston)

Tourist Information
Launceston, tel: 01566 772321

Cycle Shops/Hire
John Towl Cycles, Launceston. Tel: 01566 774220

Nearest Railway Station
Plymouth (22 miles/35.5km); Liskeard (12 miles/19km). Note: no public transport from Liskeard.

Refreshments
Pubs and cafés in Launceston. At Five Lanes the King's Head welcomes children (open all day). Launceston Steam Railway and Tamar Otter Sanctuary both have comfortable tea rooms; village stores in Canworthy Water and Altarnun.

Launceston's fine 13th-century castle was built by the brother of King Henry 111

Another Launceston attraction is its steam railway

START

Launceston is bypassed off the main A30 trunk route into Cornwall between Okehampton and Bodmin. Ample public parking and amenities near the 13th-century castle make this a good starting point.

DIRECTIONS

1. From the castle gate, drop right, downhill, following the A388 Holsworthy and Bude road (St Thomas Road). Continue over the traffic lights (turn right for Launceston Steam Railway) and up St Stephens Hill after the mini-roundabout. At the top of the hill turn left opposite the church, towards Tresmeer, Egloskerry and Canworthy Water. Admire the Bodmin skyline before branching right, signed 'Langore 0.75' after 1¼ miles (2km). Turn right at a junction 1½ miles (2.5km) after sleepy Langore, towards North Petherwin. Detour right at the main crossroads at North Petherwin for the Tamar Otter Sanctuary.

2. Back at the crossroads continue north towards Week St Mary to visit the Tamar Glass studio, just past the church. A little further on, turn left on a flat scenic country road, signed 'Canworthy Water 3.75' and continue over three T-junctions following signs to Canworthy Water. The road then climbs gently through Fonston and Warbstow Cross; turn left at the tiny Bethel Methodist Chapel towards Scarsick. A quick descent through a little valley then ascends over a redundant railway bridge (pause to absorb the farmland views). A short climb brings you to a crossroads.

3. Turn right along the dirt road

that becomes a grassy bridleway, climbing towards the pine forest. Cross the forest road continuing straight up the ill-defined grassy trail. It may be better to dismount for the incline and to avoid gorse punctures and uncleared branches on top of Wilsey Down. A silent approach may also be rewarded by fox and deer sightings. Do not deviate although the trail is almost indistingushable across the timber-strewn plateau; cross a second forest road where a blue waymarker points down through the trees again, soon emerging into a lay-by on the A395 (beware of fast traffic on this road). Proceed left along the main road for ½ mile (1km), then right towards Tregulland. Coast downhill taking in the nearby wind farm and, across to the right, Brown Willy, Bodmin Moor's highest point. Turn left at the T-junction then shortly right, through St Clether. Go left at the next T-junction, climbing through the village before turning right to Laneast. A leafy descent precedes a good rest point at the River Inny before the short steep ascent to the T-junction. Turn right, signed 'Camelford', then immediately left to Tresibbett along a quiet road with excellent views of Dartmoor. Fork left at the junction then left again, signed 'Five Lanes', descending to beautifully kept

WHAT TO LOOK OUT FOR

If you are quiet, you may glimpse foxes, deer and buzzards on forested Wilsey Down. Shortly after, technology dominates the landscape in the shape of one of Cornwall's three wind farms. In Altarnun, admire the medieval packhorse bridge and the 6th-century Celtic cross in the churchyard.

Visitors may be fortunate enough to catch sight of a shy otter at the Tamar Otter Sanctuary

Altarnun – the country of Daphne du Maurier and Jamaica Inn.

4. Beyond the fork at Five Lanes detour right to John Wesley's cottage. At the King's Head Hotel follow signs to Polyphant, passing the primary school. Remain on this road for 2 miles (3km), over a staggered crossroads to a T-junction, signed 'Davidstow and Camelford'. Turn left then soon right, over two T-junctions, signed 'Pipers Pool', to reach the A395. Turn right then quickly left at Sunny Corner Cottage towards Egloskerry; ½ mile (1km) further, branch right (do not miss it) on a bend along a little-used back road, keeping right at the next junction. From here follow Launceston signs back along the Kensey valley. When in Launceston, turn right, back up the hill to the castle and the start point of the ride.

PLACES OF INTEREST

Tamar Otter Sanctuary

This centre in North Petherwin is the only place in the West Country breeding British otters and reintroducing them into the wild. Other wildlife includes deer, waterfowl, wallabies and peacocks, and there is also a craft shop, café, picnic areas and woodland trail. Open daily, April to October, feeding times 12 noon and 3.30pm (recommended).

Altarnun

This is a very picturesque village, with slate and granite cottages and a medieval packhorse bridge. The 15th-century church, dedicated to St Nonna (mother of St David, patron saint of Wales), is sometimes referred to as the 'Cathedral of the Moors'. Of special interest are the 79 carved bench ends depicting local life and Christian symbols.

Wesley's Cottage, Trewint

Isbell Cottage was used frequently by John Wesley when on his preaching tours throughout Cornwall. Now restored and open to the public daily, it contains many artefacts relating to Wesley and the Methodist church.

John Wesley, the founder of Methodism, is closely associated with Cornwall

THE LIZARD

PENINSULA SE OF HELSTON

KYNANCE COVE

'A steep descent leads the traveller to the shore among wild and shaggy rocks where, in the scene which opens before him, he may find the glowing fancies of fairyland. The rocks appear as if they had been purposely grouped; and by their dark and varied colours pleasingly contrast with the light tints of the sandy beach and azure sea. The predominant colour of the serpentine is an olive green...divided by waving lines of red and purple...'
Murray's Handbook (1859)

The tip of the Lizard Peninsula, with its guardian lighthouse, is the furthest south you can go in England. Along the coast cliffs rising to 200ft (61m) are broken by little rocky coves, with here and there a tiny fishing village and harbour. The Lizard is known for its unique serpentine rock, predominantly green in colour. Serpentine ornaments became fashionable in Victorian times and are still made here as souvenirs. Soapstone was also extracted here. The church at Landewednack has a pulpit and lecturn made of the curious stone.

Much of the coast is cared for by the National Trust, including Mullion Cove, with its charming old harbour and island bird sanctuary, and Kynance Cove, a popular beauty spot known for its serpentine cliffs, caves and rock formations, where the sea spouts and hisses through a fissure called the Devil's Bellows. On the eastern side of the peninsula are the simple, white-washed cottages of Cadgwith and Coverack, the latter a celebrated smugglers' haven whose name is Cornish for 'hideaway'. Offshore lie the dreaded reefs of the Manacles, which have torn the life out of many a proud ship. Drowned seamen sleep their last sleep in the churchyard at St Keverne, whose tall spire was a vital landmark for ships in the Channel.

Cornwall is well-served with tales of mermaids, and a story is told of an old man at Cury, near the Lizard, who rescued a stranded mermaid and put her back in the water. He was granted three wishes and some years later, it is said, she returned for him, taking him down into the watery depths.

LOOE

TOWN ON A387, 7 MILES (11KM) S OF LISKEARD

An old port of character is set on the steep banks of the River Looe (the name rhymes with 'woo'). West Looe and East Looe, facing each other across the harbour and connected by a bridge, were separate towns until the 1880s, and each little place solemnly sent two MPs to Westminster until 1832. Cornish granite was also exported from here, including the stone to build Westminster Bridge and the Embankment in London. Most of West Looe today dates from after the arrival of the railway in 1869. East Looe is the larger and more interesting of the towns, with narrow cobbled streets and twisting alleys. Old buildings go back to the 16th century, including the Fisherman's Arms inn and the Old Guildhall, which is now a museum of local history. A popular resort with a sandy beach, East Looe developed shark fishing as a visitor attraction in the 1950s, and the Shark-sightings Club of Great Britain has its headquarters here. There are boat trips to the bird sanctuary on Looe Island, and inland up the two branches of the river. High on the cliffs to the east is the delightful Monkey Sanctuary, a breeding colony of woolly monkeys from the Amazon rain forests which fraternise amicably with visitors.

Set on the rocky coast of the Lands End peninsula with a woody backdrop, this is perhaps Cornwall's prettiest fishing village. Phoenician tin merchants came here 2,500 years ago and it is thought that the name Mousehole (pronounced 'Mowzel') may derive from their word for watering place. A little more recently, in 1595, the village fell victim to 200 Spaniards who landed here from four galleons, raping the women and burning just about all the houses bar the former manor house in Keigwin Street. Since then the village has rebuilt itself in the narrow streets and alleys that twist uphill from the curving semi-circular granite quays of the harbour.

This was once the centre of Cornwall's pilchard-fishing industry, but the pilchards had departed by the turn of the century and now only a few boats operate from here. Among the grey-brown granite houses, with their lichen-covered slate roofs and splashes of fuchsia and hydrangea, stand two large Methodist chapels, a reminder of John Wesley's activities in this area. The village church is some way up the hill; here may be found a memorial to Dolly Pentreath who died in 1777, allegedly the last person to speak – and swear – solely in Cornish. In 1981 disaster struck the village again when the Penlee lifeboat went down with its entire crew – all Mousehole men.

MOUSEHOLE

VILLAGE OFF B3315, 2 MILES (3KM) S OF PENZANCE

STARGAZY PIE

This is a local dish made with whole fish whose heads stick out through the pastry crust. Traditionally, it is eaten here on Tom Bawcock's Eve, 23 December. Tom was a Mousehole fisherman who is said to have saved the villagers from starvation after going out in a storm and bringing back a huge catch of seven different kinds of fish.

Houses cluster round the granite harbour at Mousehole

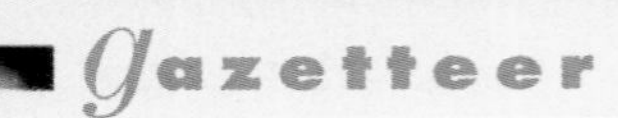

NEWLYN
TOWN ON B3315, IMMEDIATELY S OF PENZANCE

As celebrated for art as for fishing, Newlyn stands on Mount's Bay next door to Penzance. It is Cornwall's principal fishing port, and rows of houses look out over the harbour, with former sail lofts and fish cellars. A small harbour was built here in the 15th century and mackerel were always an important part of the catch – at one time each house would have had a pile of fish remains decaying noxiously outside the front door. When the railway arrived in 1859, fresh fish could be sent swiftly to London and the whole Cornish fishing industry was galvanised. The fish train left at 2pm every day, and long jetties were built out into the water to accommodate all the extra fishing boats.

A combination of the picturesque qualities of the town and the radiantly beautiful light attracted artists from the 1880s onwards, and the Newlyn School of art developed, concentrating on painting outdoors rather than formal studio work. Its leader was Stanhope Forbes, and other artists who painted here include H S Tuke, Lamorna Birch, Norman Garstin, Frank Bramley, Laura Knight and Alfred Munnings. The town is still an important centre for artists, and their work is shown in the Newlyn Art Gallery, founded in 1895 by the Cornish philanthropist Passmore Edwards.

PENTEWAN
VILLAGE ON B3273, 3 MILES (5KM) S OF ST AUSTELL

Pentewan consists of a tiny harbour and a few Regency buildings. There is a wide sandy bay lined with caravans, and a group of small green hills behind.

The Lost Gardens of Heligan
(SIGNPOSTED FROM A390 & B3273)
TEL: 01726 844157

Covering an area of 57 acres (23ha), this is the largest garden reclamation project in Britain. Four walled gardens are being restored to their former glory including the re-planting of Victorian varieties of fruit and vegetables. A feature of the garden is 'The Jungle' – a collection of palms, tree ferns and bamboo which had remained untouched for 70 years. The visitor will find plenty to see here including a New Zealand and an Italian garden, a grotto, wishing well and rockeries. Various events are held throughout the year including walks, horticultural events, theatre workshops and educational courses.

Open all year, daily. Closed 25 Dec.

PENZANCE
TOWN ON A30, 7 MILES (11KM) SW OF ST IVES

This combined market town and fishing port has grown through tourism into a large town, the most westerly in Britain. It has always been the port for ferries to the Scilly Isles, and now also houses the helicopter service. Tourism developed here from the Regency period, visitors being attracted by the very mild climate and beautiful scenery. Several Regency terraces in the west of the town survive, but business really took off after the railway arrived in the 1850s.

The centre of the town is the curving main street. In the middle is the handsome, classical domed market house of 1836, with a statue to Sir Humphry Davy (inventor of many things besides his famous lamp). Chapel Street has the best buildings, a mixture of granite and brick, with the amazing Egyptian House of 1835, chapels, inns and houses. Palms and myrtles are among the plants grown in the lush sub-tropical public gardens. The promenade to Newlyn (laid out in 1840) has a remarkable open-air pool, the 1930s Jubilee Bathing Pool, recently restored. There is a prominent 1832 church. The Penzance Museum and Art Gallery has many Newlyn School paintings, besides other local displays, and Trinity House National Lighthouse Centre has exhibits about lighthouses.

The church tower overlooks the harbour at Penzance

Maritime Museum
19 Chapel St (opposite the Admiral Benbow)
Tel: 01736 68890 & 63324 (winter/after hours)

Treasures recovered from wrecks by the diving teams of Roland Morris are on display here, including gold and silver from the first treasure found in British waters. A man-o'-war display shows a full-scale section of a 1730 warship including the gun-decks. Model ships, sailors' crafts, guns, instruments, shipwrights' tools and figureheads can also be seen.

Open Apr–Oct, daily.

PORT ISAAC
Village on B3267, 5 miles (8km) N of Wadebridge

Where the stark cliffs of the North Cornwall coast stand guard against the relentless sea between Rumps Point and Tintagel Head, the little harbour of Port Isaac is sheltered by the bulk of Lobber Point. White-washed cottages crowd the narrow streets and lanes, one of which is so cramped that it is graphically called Squeezebelly Alley. Fishing boats, nets and calling gulls lend atmosphere to a port from which Delabole slate was once shipped, before the railway arrived and took the trade away. Port Isaac was a thriving fishing harbour in the 19th century when the vast shoals of pilchard made their regular appearances along the Cornish coast. They come no more, and the little town depends on visitors for its living today; however, the fish cellars used for salting pilchards can still be seen. The handsome old parish church is to the south at St Endellion, and a couple of miles to the east rise the double ramparts (up to 50ft/15m wide) of Tregeare Rounds.

The picturesque fishing harbour at Port Isaac

This Celtic hill fort was excavated in 1904, and pottery dating from shortly before the Roman period was discovered. The fort has been identified as the Castle Terrible of Thomas Malory's 15th-century epic *Morte D'Arthur* – the spot where Uther Pendragon besieged the Duke of Cornwall.

Delabole Slate Quarry
On B3314, 2 miles (3km) W of Camelford

Slate has been quarried since the 14th century at this village near Port Isaac, and the huge quarry, 500ft (153m) deep and more than ½ mile (1km) across, is still in use (viewing platform). The sails for the new wind farm for generating electricity are prominent. The village expanded with the quarrying, and is mostly 19th-century.

SCILLY, ISLES OF

See Isles of Scilly, page 64.

An exhilarating coastal walk through National Trust property, with glorious views of the North Cornish coast and the Camel Estuary; the route includes a circuit of an Iron Age fortified headland.

Grid ref: SW41799

INFORMATION

The walk is just over 4miles (6.5km) long.
Walking is generally easy, with some short, steep sections.
No stiles, but several gates.
Dogs must be under strict control where sheep are grazing; dogs are banned on local beaches from Easter to September.
Take care with children where the path skirts the cliff edge.
Wooden seats along the way and grassy areas on The Rumps provide good picnic spots.
Toilets and refreshments at New Polzeath.

START

From Wadebridge take the B3314 and follow signs for New Polzeath. At a crossroads ½ mile (1km) before New Polzeath, turn right down a narrow lane to Pentireglaze. Follow the road where it bends left in front of some cottages, go over a cattle grid and 200yds (183m) ahead, turn right into a National Trust car park.

DIRECTIONS

Leave the car park by the back corner, where there is an information panel and National Trust collecting box. Go up a stony path, then keep alongside a wall to reach a gate in the opposite field corner.

Beyond the gate, turn left along the coast path, taking particular care for the first 50yds (46m) where the path is close to the cliff edge. Keep to the main coast path for about ¼ mile (0.5km) to reach the double-headed promontory of The Rumps, where the defensive embankments of Iron Age fortifications still survive.

The Rumps seen from Cliff Castle

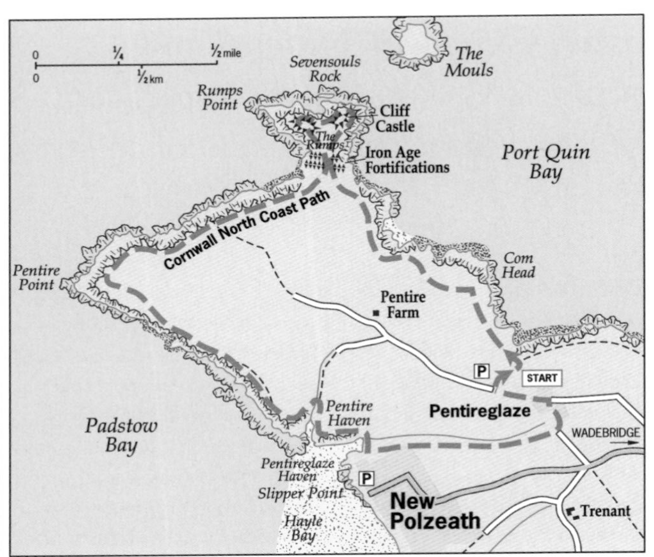

A circuit of the promontory can be made by following the path along its eastern edge, from where there are splendid views of Mouls Island just offshore. Take care on steeper slopes. Leave The Rumps by the entrance gap in the embankment, then follow the the broad track that runs right and uphill to where it merges with an upper path. Continue to a gate, level with a trig point, and pass through. Where the path forks beyond the gate, take the right-hand branch to Pentire Point.

Just before the Point, turn left, follow the low wall, and continue along the coast path for ¼ mile (0.5km). Pass above the narrow inlet of Pentire Haven (short rocky descent) and continue along the coast path to Pentireglaze Haven. At the far side of Pentireglaze Haven beach, turn left along a wide track, passing a house on your left. Where the track loops back to the right, keep straight ahead along a grassier track, then straight on through fields, passing through several gates, to a road. Turn left, walk through Pentireglaze, and follow the track left to return to the car park.

Mining

Mining figures strongly in the history of Cornwall, and lead was mined near Pentireglaze from the 16th to the 19th century. The National Trust car park actually lies within spoil heaps from an old lead mine.

The Rumps

The headland is a classic example of an Iron Age promontory site, fortified across its narrow neck by banks and ditches. Wooden huts would have been situated just inside the entranceway. The site was probably established some time after 500 BC and abandoned by the middle of the 1st century AD.

Pentire Point

In 1936, the glorious western slopes of Pentire Point above the Camel Estuary were divided into building plots and put up for sale. Conservationists, both locally and nationally, raised sufficient money to buy the headland and then presented it to the National Trust, with the intention of ensuring preservation and public access for future generations.

WHAT TO LOOK OUT FOR

Goldfinches, stonechats and whitethroats are common here, and kestrels hang motionless in the updraught above the cliffs. On the western side of Pentire Point, oystercatchers throng the tidal rocks, and seals may be spotted in the restless waters near The Rumps. In spring and summer the cliff slopes are vivid with pink thrift, white bladder campion, and the lovely pale blue squill.

ST AUSTELL
TOWN ON A390, 13 MILES (20KM) NE OF TRURO

This was a town based on quarrying and mining tin and copper from early times, and on china clay after its discovery here in 1748 by the Plymouth chemist William Cookworthy. The 'Cornish Alps' (or 'White Alps') to the north of the town are waste tips of gritty quartz, by-products of the quarrying. China clay is today used for paper, paints, medicines, plastics, cosmetics and toothpaste, as well as for china. The 'Alps' are now being reclaimed and made green; the older ones, with trees, are beginning to look like natural, if steep hills.

The town is not large, and still has some older parts. The central church has a superb late 15th-century tower and wooden roofs of the same date. Buildings include the very plain granite Quaker meeting house of 1829, and the simple market hall of 1844. The St Austell Brewery, which started in the late 19th century, has a visitor centre and gives guided tours.

Charlestown Shipwreck & Heritage Centre
QUAY RD, CHARLESTOWN (1.25M SE OF A3061)
TEL: 01726 69897 & 68025

Charlestown is a small and unspoilt village with a unique sea-lock china-clay port. It was purpose-built in the 18th century by Charles Rashleigh. The Shipwreck and Heritage Centre houses the largest display of shipwreck artefacts in the UK, along with a series of lifesize tableaux and photographs depicting village life, an audio-visual describing the local heritage, a Scarborough Lifeboat and a lifeboat display. An important 'History of Diving' display is a recent addition to the Centre, which currently hosts the 'Mary Rose' travelling exhibition.

Open Mar–Oct, daily. Last admission 1 hour before closing. Bookings taken out of season.

St Austell's church tower, seen from Fore Street

ST IVES

Town on A3074, 7 miles (11km) NE of Penzance

Until the 1890s the prosperity of this picturesque town was based on pilchards and tin, but this century the emphasis has changed to tourism and art. Beautifully situated, with sandy beaches on either side and a rocky headland in the middle, the town itself is small-scale and well preserved, with little cobbled streets, flowers everywhere, many external staircases and steep alleyways. Fishing boats still use the harbour, and the town museum is close by.

Out on the headland is the little Chapel of St Michael, and in the town is the early 15th-century St Ia's Church, with a Madonna and Child by Barbara Hepworth, who lived here.

From the late 19th century St Ives attracted artists, but the St Ives colony dates from the 1930s, with Hepworth and Ben Nicholson the earliest members, along with Bernard Leach, who established his pottery at Upper Stennack, high in the town, in the 1920s. The Tate Gallery displays modern art created in Cornwall in its striking modern (1993) building in Porthmeor beach, a spot popular with surfers.

A park and ride service is available at Lelant Station.

Barbara Hepworth Museum & Sculpture Garden

Barnoon Hill

Tel: 01736 796226

The artist Turner visited St Ives in 1811. Then, after the railway was established in 1880, the town became a popular haunt for artists; what was once a busy fishing port took on a distinctly Bohemian atmosphere as the net-lofts and fish-cellars were converted into studios. The house and garden that Dame Barbara Hepworth called home from 1949 until her death in 1975 is now a museum displaying 47 sculptures and drawings covering the period 1928–74, as well as photographs, documents and other memorabilia. Visitors can also visit her workshops, which house a selection of tools and some unfinished carvings. The museum is administered jointly with the Tate Gallery St Ives.

Open all year Apr–Oct daily, Nov–Mar, Tue–Sun. Closed 24–26 Dec.

An exhibit in the Sculpture Garden at the museum

Tate Gallery St Ives
Porthmeor Beach
Tel: 01736 796226

This gallery presents changing displays from the Tate Gallery's collections of modern art related to Cornwall covering the years c1925–75. There are also temporary exhibitions of work by contemporary artists, please telephone for details.

Open all year; Apr–Oct daily, Nov–Mar Tue–Sun. Closed 24–26 Dec.

ST MICHAEL'S MOUNT
Island in Mount's Bay, ½ mile (1km) offshore from Marazion
Accessible by causeway at low tide
Tel: 01736 710507

The famous romantic view is of the fairy-tale castle (National Trust) perched on top of the rocky island dominating Mount's Bay, joined to the mainland by a causeway at low tide, and by ferries from Marazion at high tide. The village at the bottom, with its harbour, is beautifully preserved.

An old Cornish legend claims that in the 5th century some fishermen saw the Archangel Michael on a ledge of rock on the western side of the Mount, and it has been called St Michael's Mount ever since. The legend of Jack the Giant-Killer also originated here: the giant Cormoran was said to have built the Mount, from where he waded ashore to steal cows and sheep from the locals. Jack rowed out to the Mount one night and dug a great pit while the giant slept. The next morning Cormoran awoke and set off towards the shore, but fell into the pit – which is still shown to children who visit the Mount.

In ancient times St Michael's Mount may well have been the Isle of Ictis, which was known to Greek travellers and merchants. It was for many years an important port, not only for the export of Cornish tin, but also for trade in Irish gold and copper.

Legends aside, this great rock is a picturesque sight. Perched upon its summit is a building which has been a church, a priory, a fortress and a private home. It was built in 1135 by the abbot of its namesake, Mont St Michel in Normandy, to whom it had been granted by the Norman Earl of Cornwall. However, the original building was destroyed by an earthquake in 1275. It was difficult, with their French connection, for the monks of St Michael's Mount to prosper during the intervening years as England was constantly at war with France.

For all its isolation, the Mount was seen as strategically important whenever there was turmoil in the country – the Wars of the Roses, the Prayer Book Rebellion, the Armada and, of course, the Civil War, when it was a Royalist stronghold until it surrendered to Parliament in 1646, and was subsequently taken over as a garrison.

When the military left, the Mount came into the private ownership of the St Aubyn family, but in the days when travel was arduous and social connections were paramount it left much to be desired as a dwelling. In fact, the Mount remained largely unoccupied, used only occasionally during the summer, until the late 18th century when the family began to look upon the Mount as a more permanent residence.

Undaunted by the fact that the living quarters were not of an adequate size, they set about the construction of a great new wing

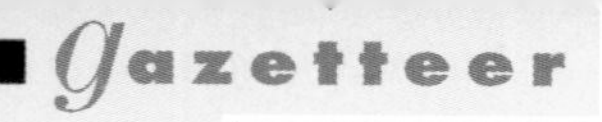

– clearly not an easy task on a great rock which is cut off by every high tide.

The St Aubyns were a force to be reckoned with and the splendid Victorian apartments that they added are as much a testament to their determination as to their good taste. There are some fine plaster reliefs, beautiful Chippendale furniture and collections of armour and pictures.

Open Apr–Oct on weekdays.

TINTAGEL
Village on B3263, 4 miles (6.5km) NW of Camelford

Geoffrey of Monmouth, in about 1150, was responsible for spreading the idea that a fortress here had been the birthplace of King Arthur in the 6th century. The legend has flourished ever since and became especially popular in the Romantic era of the 19th century, when visitors started to flock here. Now, in summer, the place is a tourist honeypot, but if you come out of season, the magic cannot fail to work. Tintagel village, originally called Trevena, was one of several villages in the parish of Tintagel that grew up, like others, round its manor house. This rare 14th-century building, known as the Old Post Office, is sturdily built with tiny windows in its dark stone walls and a roof of heavy uneven slates. But everything else in the village is insubstantial; what is important is 'the island', a precipitous promontory joined to the cliffs by a narrow neck of land. It is an impressive sight, lonely and windswept, the waters of the Atlantic swirling relentlessly far below. There are the remains of what some consider to be 6th-century monastic cells, others a tin-trading settlement, but more prominent are the black ruins of a castle built from the 12th century onwards by Norman earls of Cornwall to keep watch on the Celts. All too easily the romance of the place takes over and they become in our imagination the ruins of Arthur's castle.

On one side lay the Ocean, and on one
Lay a great water, and the moon was full.
Tennyson, 'The Passing of Arthur'

The Old Post Office
Tel: 01840 770024

This 14th-century manor-house served as a receiving office for letters from 1844 to 1892; it is now in the care of the National Trust.

Open Apr–Oct, daily.

Tintagel Castle
On Tintagel Head, ½ mile (1km) along uneven track from Tintagel, no vehicles.
Tel: 01840 770328

In the winter, ferocious storms whip up around the rugged Cornish coast, wearing away at the rocky peninsula that is home to the scanty remains of Tintagel Castle. Each year parts are swept away, and so what remains today is not what would have existed when Reginald, an illegitimate son of Henry I, first raised his castle here.

Tintagel is traditionally associated with the legend of King Arthur, who, it is said, was conceived here while Merlin waited in a cave under the castle. The cave that pierces the thin neck of rock which joins the peninsula to the mainland is still called Merlin's Cave, and it can

The caves in the headland at Tintagel have been the inspiration for legends

be visited at low tide. This is a wild and desolate place, where it is easy to imagine the romantic image of the legendary hero, but there is no concrete evidence to support the connection.

About 100 years after Reginald had built his square hall, Richard, Earl of Cornwall, built two more enclosures and raised some walls. The Black Prince built another hall, and there is evidence that yet another was raised over the remains of the previous two. Archaeologically, Tintagel is difficult to understand, and there are foundations of buildings and several tunnels, the purpose of which remains unknown – all adding to the castle's air of mystery.

Open all year. Closed 24–26 Dec. Please note there is a steep climb up steps to reach the castle.

TREDINNICK SHIRE HORSE CENTRE

Trelow Farm, off A39, 4 miles (6.5km) SW of Wadebridge

Tel: 01841 540276

This 120-acre (49-ha) farm specialises in Shire horses, and visitors can see mares with foals. There are two horse shows a day which take place under cover and are fully seated, and cart rides are also available. The work of the blacksmith is also on display and there is a museum of carriages, a video room and the largest display of show harnesses in the country. The unique owl sanctuary enables owls to fly freely in a twilight atmosphere. There is a children's world of adventure playground, and small animals and special rare breeds can be seen.

Open Good Fri–Oct daily. Closed Sat in Oct.

This pleasant and varied route weaves its way through quiet Cornish countryside, passing medieval churches, a prehistoric hill fort and the ruins of an Iron-Age village (see also page 60). There are long level stretches with some moderate uphill sections and only one or two short steep sections. The ride is mainly on quiet country lanes, but has a main road start and two quite busy crossings en route.

INFORMATION

Total Distance
19 miles (30.5 km)

Difficulty
Moderate

OS Map
Landranger 1:50,000 sheet 203 (Lands End, The Lizard & Isles of Scilly)

Tourist Information
Penzance. Tel: 01736 62207

Cycle Shops/Hire
Blewett and Pender, Albert Street, Penzance. Tel: 01736 64157; The Cycle Centre, Bread Street,

The remains of the Iron-Age settlement at Chysauster

Penzance. Tel: 01736 51671; Geoff's Bikes, Victoria Place, Penzance. Tel: 01736 63665

Nearest Railway Station:
Penzance

Refreshments:
There are pubs at Gulval, Crowlas, St Erth, Hayle Causeway, Cripplesease and Nancledra. They all serve food and welcome children. Places to sample those famous Cornish cream teas include *The Wink* tea rooms at Cripplesease. There are plenty of picnic spots on the right bank of the River Hayle at St Erth.

START

Penzance, on the A30, 24 miles (38.5km) south-west of Truro, is a lively market town and port facing Mount's Bay. You should normally be able to park at the large pay-and-display harbour car park near the railway station.

DIRECTIONS

1 Turn left out of the harbour car park then, after a few yards, left again into the one-way system and filter right onto the lane marked 'A30, Redruth'. (This first short section is unavoidably busy with traffic, so take care, especially with youngsters.) Follow the one-way system round to the right, filtering to the left-hand lane, to reach traffic lights. Continue along the A30 out of Penzance for about ¼ mile (0.5km) to a large roundabout. Take the second exit, signed 'Heliport', then go immediately right, again signposted 'Heliport'. In ¼ mile (0.5km) turn left into a quiet lane, signed 'Gulval', which is reached after ¼ mile (0.5km). The Coldstreamer Inn is up to the left. Turn right at Gulval and follow a narrow lane for 2 miles (3km). Turn right at a T-junction, signed 'Crowlas', and pass the Old Inn, soon to reach a junction with the A30. There are shops and the Star Inn down to the left.

Shopping in Penzance on Causeway Head

2 Taking care, cross the A30 then continue down the lane opposite for 1 mile (1.5km). Turn left, signed 'St Erth', and continue along a pleasant level lane for 3 miles (5km) to reach St Erth. (There are roadside toilets just before the St Erth Bridge.) Directly up the steep hill from the bridge is the Star Inn. From the far side of the St Erth Bridge turn left, signed 'Hayle', and in 1 mile (1.5km), passing a pitch and putt course, reach the B3301.

Fields near the Minions, the site of many ancient monuments

3 Turn left, signed 'St Ives', and continue along a busy section of road known as Hayle Causeway. It is bounded by Lelant Saltings, the head of Hayle Estuary, on the right and by a wide footpath on the left. After 220 yards (200m) filter right with care and cross the right-hand carriageway on to a side road, signed 'Carbis Bay'. Pass the Old Quay House Inn and continue along the side road, for 600 yards (550m) to reach a roundabout. Keep right, signed 'Holiday Route', then at the next roundabout take the first exit left signed 'Holiday Route'. Pass the Watermill Restaurant on the right and continue steadily uphill (not steep) for 1 mile (1.5km). On a right-hand bend proceed left on to the first of two side roads (not signposted). Climb steadily for ½ mile (1km) to reach the National Trust's Trencom Hill car park, shielded by bushes on the right. Continue along a delightful lane for 1 mile (1.5km). Pass a junction with a large grassy central triangle. (The route goes left here, but a short distance straight ahead is a junction with the B3311. About 150 yards (123m) up to the right from this junction, at Cripplesease, is the Engine Inn and, opposite the junction, The Wink tea room offering cream teas.)

4 Continue down the narrow lane from the grassy triangle. Pass an old mine engine house on the left and a Cornish cross on the right. Continue straight across at a crossroads and make a steep descent, with care, through

WHAT TO LOOK OUT FOR

West Cornwall's characteristic laneside 'hedges', which are stone walls smothered with vegetation, are a riot of colour in spring and summer. Primroses, celandines, wild garlic, pennywort, foxgloves along with polypody fern and mosses and lichens, are just some of the species. Buzzards and kestrels hover above the small inland valleys and, at Hayle Estuary, there are wading birds on the mudflats at low tide, or riding on the water at high tide. Lelant Saltings provides important feeding grounds for migratory and resident birds.

twisting bends. Soon, cross a bridge, turn right at a T-junction and continue for 380 yards (350m) to reach a junction with the B3311. Turn left here through a tight corner followed by a brief incline. Continue for 2 miles (3km). On the left there are outstanding views of Mount's Bay and St Michael's Mount. At Badger's Cross turn right, signed 'Chysauster', and continue along a level lane for 1½ miles (2.5km), still following signs to Chysauster. Reach the Chysauster car park (toilets). The ancient Chysauster Iron Age village is up to the right.

5 From Chysauster car park, continue along the lane for 1 mile (1.5km). Watch out for occasional vehicles on the bends. Climb a short steep section, then descend steeply to a T-junction. Turn left, signed 'Penzance'. Go through New Mill and continue for 2 miles (3km), with one short steep section, to reach another T-junction. Go left here, signed 'Penzance', and after 300 yards (270m) join the B3311, keeping right, signed 'Penzance'. In 500 yards (460m) reach a junction with the A30. Turn right here, with care, and soon return to Penzance station and the harbour car park.

PLACES OF INTEREST

Gulval

This charming, flower-filled village is clustered around a 15th-century church, itself encircled by trees and exotic shrubs. Most of Gulval's fine houses and cottages are Victorian and built of excellent granite. The Coldstreamer Inn is reached by the lane to the left of the church.

St Erth

The River Hayle flows serenely through St Erth. The delightful church, which dates from the 14th century, has been restored over the centuries. A steep little lane leads up to the village centre.

Trencom Hill

This prominent hill is 550ft (167m) high and has a flat top and vestiges of the embankments that once made it a major hill fort of the Iron Age. There are magnificent views from the top, which is reached on foot by a short but steep climb from a National Trust car park.

The fine 14th-century church at St Erth and the River Hayle

TRELISSICK GARDEN
TEL: 01872 862090 & 865808

A beautiful woodland park of some 370 acres (150ha) overlooking the Fal estuary. The park was mainly laid out between 1844 and 1913 but the gardens were designed later, between 1937 and 1955. The grounds have been immaculately kept and offer spectacular views from walks through beech trees and oaks.

The location of the garden, near the sea and sheltered by woodland, has allowed many unusual and exotic plants to be grown. There are sub-tropical plants, some from such distant places as Chile and Tasmania. The gardens are particularly noted for their camellias, magnolias and hydrangeas, of which there are over 100 kinds. There is also a large walled garden with fig trees and climbers, and a shrub garden. Plants are available in the garden shop. There is also an Art and Craft Gallery by the House Farm Courtyard.

Open Mar–Oct, Mon–Sat, Sun afternoons. Restaurant open afternoons. Woodland walks open Nov–Feb.

TRURO
CITY OFF A39, 13 MILES (21KM) SW OF ST AUSTELL

The county town of Cornwall was a medieval stannary town where tin was taken to be weighed and taxed, and the principal port for tin. It became a city in 1887, and a huge new cathedral was designed in 1880 by J L Pearson, the first Anglican cathedral to be built in England since St Paul's in London.

The wide river was used for cargo transport into the 20th century and now has an attractive walk beside it. The Royal Cornwall Museum has extensive displays on the county.

Truro's great cathedral catches the eye from all quarters. It rises from the heart of the city, its honey-coloured stone and lancet windows reflecting the sun, its great Gothic towers piercing the sky. There is no trace of the Norman castle that once stood at Truro, nor of the Dominican friary that stood near the low ground by the river, but the cathedral makes up for their loss.

A short distance away is the Crown Court, a stylish building designed by the same architects who were responsible for the St Ives Tate Gallery (see page 81). Below here are the pleasant Victoria Gardens. Boscawen Park, by the Truro River, is reached along the road to Malpas. The art gallery has works by John Opie, the 18th-century portrait painter who was born near St Agnes.

Truro's fortunes rose and fell over the years, but by the late 18th century it had become the political and cultural centre of Georgian Cornwall. It was during the last years of the 18th century that such famous features as Boscawen Street and Lemon Street were built. Today Boscawen Street is a broad, cobbled space, entered at both ends from narrow thoroughfares. The granite façade of the City Hall still graces Boscawen Street, and Lemon Street survives as one of the

WOODLAND WALKS
North of Truro, at Idless, is Bishop's Wood, a pleasant Forestry Commission plantation of mainly conifers but with a mix of broadleaved trees such as birch, hazel and willow. The wood can be reached by driving north from Truro on the B3284 to Shortlanesend, from where side roads lead to Idless. There is a car park at the edge of the wood just north of Idless. The wood is criss-crossed with broad forest tracks and there is a pleasant walk alongside a busy little stream.

finest examples of a late Georgian street in Britain, its houses perfectly aligned to either side of a broad avenue that climbs gracefully uphill.

There are hidden glories in Truro amidst the cruder modern developments. From the functional harshness of the Moorfield car park, a cramped lane leads to Victoria Square, but parallel and to its right is the elegant Georgian crescent of Walsingham Place. Throughout the heart of Truro alleyways and lanes connect the main streets and are lined with attractive shops, cafés and restaurants. From the west end of Boscawen Street, King Street leads up to the pedestrianised area of High Cross in front of the cathedral. The stylish Assembly Rooms, with a façade of Bath stone, stand near by.

Seen from its forecourt the cathedral seems crowded in by surrounding buildings, whereas from outside the city it commands the view. But the west front and its soaring towers are exhilarating. The foundation stones of the cathedral were laid in 1880 and the western towers were finally dedicated in 1920; thus it is a Victorian building,

Completed in 1910, Truro's magnificent cathedral is relatively modern

Early English Gothic in design but with strong French influences that are seen in the great spires. The interior is glorious, vaulted throughout with pillars and arches in the most elegant proportions and the air is light beneath the great roofs. There are beautiful individual features such as the exquisite baptistry. All that remains of the old parish church of St Mary's is incorporated into the cathedral's south aisle.

Those with an eye for ancient stonework may find the outer wall of the old church a reassuring contrast to the rather smooth planes of the Victorian cathedral. Pydar Street runs north from the cathedral as a pleasant concourse but loses its identity at a busy junction.

Royal Cornwall Museum
River St (follow A390 towards town centre)
Tel: 01872 72205

The museum has interesting and well laid out displays on Cornish history, and also houses a world-famous collection of minerals. There are paintings and drawings, including a number of Old Masters, and some excellent exhibits of pottery, pewter, Japanese ivories, lacquerwork and toys. An extension houses two temporary exhibition galleries and a café. Other galleries house displays of mining and minerals, archaeology, Cornish history, and Egyptian artefacts.

Open all year, Mon–Sat. Closed BH.

WADEBRIDGE
Town off A389, 6 miles (10km) NW of Bodmin

A market town on the Camel estuary, with one of the finest medieval bridges in the country; the bridge was built by Thomas Lovibond in about 1468 and is 320ft (97m) long. It originally had 17 arches, and is known as 'The Bridge of the Wool', for the pillars are believed to have been built on packs of wool laid down as a foundation to hold the shifting sand of the river. The town also boasts some Victorian architecture. Wadebridge was once a busy port importing coal, timber and limestone, while exporting iron and china clay. The Royal Cornwall Show is held here annually.

WENDRON
Village on B3297, 2 miles (3km) N of Helston

This somewhat bleak hamlet, in a once-busy mining area, has a late medieval granite church with an unusual room over the lych-gate. Near by is the Poldark Mine which is well worth a visit.

Poldark Mine and Heritage Complex
Tel: 01326 573173

This Cornish tin mine has three levels open to the public, an 18th-century village, museums and a cinema showing a film on the history of Cornish mining. On the surface there are restaurants, shops, gardens and children's amusements. The area around the mine has been laid to lawn and shows the West Country's largest collection of antiquities, including a 40-ft beam engine.

Open Etr–Oct, daily.

Wacker Quay picnic site lies on the south bank of the meandering, scenic Lynher River, a short ferry-ride across Plymouth Sound. A small, secluded spot offering lovely views of the creeks and the river, it is an ideal starting place for exploring this unspoiled stretch of the Cornish coast.

HOW TO GET THERE

Take the Torpoint ferry from Devonport, crossing the county border from Devon into Cornwall, and follow the A374. One mile (1.5km) beyond Antony there is a signposted lay-by to the right. A short, steep lane leads from here down to the creek.

FACILITIES

Small, sheltered, grassy clearing, right on the riverbank.
Several picnic tables.
Small, stony beach for launching private canoes and small sailing craft.

Wacker Quay is situated on the edge of a picturesque creek, sheltered by ancient oak trees, and set against a backdrop of lush, rolling countryside. The grassy riverbank, scattered with picnic tables, affords the perfect opportunity to launch small craft for exploring the Lynher, which joins four other rivers to form one of the world's finest natural harbours.

Cornish heritage

A short distance from Wacker Quay are numerous sites of historical interest. Antony House, a beautifully proportioned Queen Anne house owned by the National Trust, between Antony and Torpoint, is one of the most distinguished country houses in Cornwall. Near by, the 16th-century Mount Edgcumbe House attracts visitors to its gardens, coastal walk, deer park and sweeping views across Plymouth Sound.

The road to the small village of St Germans is particularly scenic. Once the seat of the Anglo-Saxon

Wacker Quay is a delightful location for a picnic site

bishops of Cornwall from 936 to 1043, its ancient church boasts a splendid porch, one of the finest relics of Norman architecture in England.

A smugglers' coastline

South of Wacker Quay is Rame Head, the most easterly headland of Cornwall and crowned by a small ruined chapel, with exceptional views extending from the surfing beach of Whitsand Bay to Lizard Point. The fishing villages of Kingsand and Cawsand, with their brightly painted, crooked cottages tumbling down narrow lanes to the sea, were once famous for their safe anchorage (Nelson often stayed at the Ship Inn here). There was a thriving pilchard industry, as well as one of the largest smuggling fleets in the West Country. Today, sailing dinghies and sunbathers have taken the place of the smugglers' luggers on the secluded sandy beaches.

The sea nearly surrounds the chapel that sits on the top pf Rame Head

Close by

A short ferry crossing takes you to Plymouth with its varied attractions. Further to the west is the lively port of Looe and the picture-postcard village of Polperro with its fascinating Smuggling Museum.

West Penwith is Celtic Cornwall at its most inspiring, a patch of England on which modern man has left little mark. The weathered, grey buildings of the village of Zennor huddle together in a dip in this ancient granite landscape, lumps of stone strewn around, trees struggling to beat the gales. The church is Norman and medieval but much altered, and is chiefly known for the 15th-century bench-end, now part of a chair, on which is carved the famous mermaid of Zennor who, according to legend, lured the squire's son down down to her home beneath the waves. The Wayside Museum depicts the industrial past of the area, also reflected in the name of the pub, the Tinners' Arms, where D H Lawrence drank while living near by during World War I, at work on his novel *Women in Love*. To the north-west of the village are the jagged cliffs of Zennor Head, with rugged stretches of coastline on either side. Just inland, up on the bleak, treeless moorland, is Zennor Quoit, a Neolithic chambered tomb with a capstone 18ft (5.5m) long that was supported on five upright stones until vandalised by farmers in the 19th century. One end now rests on the ground. All around, in the bracken and gorse, are field boundary walls built long ago by Iron Age farmers.

Zennor's Wayside Folk Museum is the oldest private museum in Cornwall, founded in 1935, and covers every aspect of life in Zennor and the surrounding district from 3,000BC to the 1930s. Over 5,000 items are displayed in twelve workshops and rooms covering wheelwrights, blacksmiths, agriculture, fishing, wrecks, mining, domestic and archaeological artefacts. A photographic exhibition entitled 'People of Past Zennor' tells the story of the village and its people. The Miller's Cottage has a kitchen, parlour, mill and three working waterwheels. The delightful gardens are bounded on one side by a river. The majority of displays are under cover.

Open Apr–Sep, daily; Oct, Sun–Fri.

ZENNOR

Village on B3306, 4 miles (6.5km) W of St Ives

The legend of the Mermaid is carved on a bench-end

'A tiny granite village nestling under high shaggy moor-hills, and a big sweep of lovely sea beyond, such a lovely sea, lovelier ever than the Mediterranean...It is all gorse now, flickering with flowers; and then it will be the heather; and then hundreds of foxgloves. It is the best place I have been in, I think.'

D H Lawrence, writing to John Middleton Murray and Katherine Mansfield from Zennor, March 1916

Wayside Folk Museum
Tel: 01736 796945

LISTINGS

CONTACTS AND ADDRESSES

CORNWALL TOURIST INFORMATION CENTRES

Fowey, The Ticket Shop,Post Office, 4 Custom House Hill. Tel: 01726 833616.

Looe,The Guildhall, Fore St, East Looe. Tel: 01503 262072 (Open Easter - Oct).

Lostwithel, Community Centre, Liddicoat Road. Tel: 01208 872207.

Cornwall Wildlife Trust, Five Acres, Allet, Truro. Tel: 01872 73939

National Rivers Authority, Marley House, Kestrel Way, Exeter. Tel: 01392 444000

National Trust For Cornwall, Cornwall Regional Office, Lanhydrock, Bodmin. Tel: 01208 74281

Bodmin, Shire House, Mount Folly Square. Tel: 01208 76616

Bude, The Crescent Car Park. Tel: 01288 354240

Camelford, North Cornwall Museum, The Clease. Tel: 01840 212954

Launceston, Market House Arcade, Market Street. Tel: 01566 772321

Padstow , North Quay. Tel: 01841 533449

Mevagissey, 8 Tregoney Hill. Tel: 01726 842266

Newquay, Municipal Buildings, Marcus Hill. Tel: 01637 871345

Perranporth, Perranporth. Tel: 01872 573368

St Austell,Bypass Service Station, Southbourne Road. Tel: 01726 76333

Falmouth, 28 Killigrew Street. Tel: 01326 312300

Helston, 79 Meneage Street. Tel: 01326 565431

St Ives, The Guildhall, Street-an-Pol. Tel: 01736 796297

Penzance, Station Road. Tel: 01736 62207

Hayle, Putting Green, Lethlean Lane (seasonal).

St Mary's, Porthcressa Bank, Hugh Town. Tel: 01720 422536

DEVON TOURIST INFORMATION CENTRES

Barnstaple,Central Library, Tully Street. Tel: 01271 388583

Bideford, The Quay. Tel: 01237 477676

Combe Martin, Sea Cottage, Cross Street (seasonal). Tel: 01271 883319

Ilfracombe, The Promenade. Tel: 01271 863001

Lynton & Lynmouth, Town Hall, Lynton. Tel: 01598 752225

Devon Wildlife Trust, Shirehampton House, 35–37 St David's Hill, Exeter. Tel: 01392 79244

English Heritage Historic Properties South-West, 7/8 King Street, Bristol BS1 4EQ. Tel: 0117 9750700

Forestry Commission, South West England Conservancy Office, Avon Fields, Somerdale, Keynsham, Bristol. Tel: 0117 9869481

National Trust for Devon, Killerton House, Broadclyst, Exeter. Tel: 01208 74287

Nature Conservancy Council, The Old Mill House, 37 North Street, Okehampton. Tel: 01837 55045

Crediton, Market Street Car Park. Tel: 01363 772006

South Molton, Information Centre, 1 East Street. (seasonal) Tel : 01769 574122.

Tiverton, Phoenix Lane. Tel: 01884 255827

Ivybridge, South Dartmoor Tourist Information Centre, Leonards Road. Tel: 01752 897035

Okehampton, Museum Courtyard, 3 West Street (seasonal). Tel: 01837 53020

Plymouth, Civic Centre, Royal Parade. Tel: 01752 264849

Tavistock, Town Hall, Bedford Square. Tel: 01822 612938

Brixham, The Old Market House, The Quay. Tel: 01803 852861

Dartmouth, The Engine House, Mayor's Avenue. Tel: 01803 834224

Dawlish, The Lawn. Tel: 01626 863589

Kingsbridge, The Quay. Tel: 01548 853195

Paignton, The Esplanade. Tel: 01803 558363

Salcombe, Council Hall, Market Street. Tel: 01548 843927

Teignmouth, The Den. Tel: 01626 779769/778333

Torquay, Vaughan Parade. Tel: 01803 297428

Totnes, The Plains. Tel: 01803 863168

Axminster, The Old Courthouse, Church Street. Tel: 01297 34386

Budleigh Salterton, Fore Street. Tel: 01395 445275

Exeter, Civic Centre. Tel: 01392 265700

Exmouth, Alexandra Terrace. Tel: 01395 263744

Honiton, Dowell Street East Car Park. Tel 01404 43716

Ottery St Mary, Tel: 01404 813964

Sidmouth, Ham Lane. Tel: 01395 516441

INDEX

ACKNOWLEDGEMENTS

The Automobile Association wishes to thank the following photographers and libraries for their assistance in the preparation of this book.

THE MANSELL COLLECTION 71

The remaining photographs are held in the Association's own library (AA PHOTO LIBRARY) and were taken by:
A Baker 93; P Baker 6, 9, 16, 19, 20, 25, 27, 37, 39, 40/1, 42, 46/7, 50, 51, 53, 66; A Lawson 13, 29, 73, 75, 80;
S&O Matthews 4; R Moss 12, 14/5, 33, 44, 55, 57, 59, 61, 64, 69, 76, 79, 85, 89, 92; T Teegan 10, 83.

Cover photographs: INTERNATIONAL PHOTOBANK: back – top
ANDY WILLIAMS PHOTO LIBRARY: front – main
STEVE WATKINS/NATURAL EXPOSURE: front – cyclists
A Baker: back – middle; A Lawson: back – bottom